Brown Bag
Success

Brown Bag Success: Making Healthy Lunches Your Kids
Won't Trade © 1997 by Sandra Nissenberg, M.S., R.D.,
and Barbara Pearl, M.S., R.D.

Library of Congress Cataloging-in-Publication Data

Sandra Nissenberg, M.S., R.D., and Barbara Pearl, M.S.,
R.D. Brown bag success / by Sandra Nissenberg, M.S.,
R.D., and Barbara Pearl, M.S., R.D.

p.   cm.

Includes index.

ISBN 1-56561-123-3; $9.95

Edited by: Jolene Steffer
Cover Design: Graven Images
Text Design & Production: David Enyeart
Art/Production Manager: Claire Lewis
Printed in the United States

Published by
Chronimed Publishing
P.O. Box 59032
Minneapolis, MN 55459-0032

10   9   8   7   6   5   4   3   2   1

Brown Bag Success

Making Healthy Lunches
Your Kids Won't Trade

Sandra K. Nissenberg, M.S., R.D.

and

Barbara N. Pearl, M.S., R.D.

CHRONIMED PUBLISHING

About the Authors

Sandra K. Nissenberg, M.S., R.D. is a nutrition consultant in Buffalo Grove, Illinois. She is also coauthor of *How Should I Feed My Child?*, *Quick Meals for Healthy Kids and Busy Parents*, *Foods to Stay Vibrant, Young and Healthy* and editor of *The Healthy Start Kids Cookbook*.

Barbara N. Pearl, M.S., R.D. practices nutrition counseling in Buffalo Grove, Illinois. She instructs individuals of all ages, as well as entire families. She also teaches nutrition classes to elementary and junior high school students. Prior to starting her private practice, Barbara was the pediatric/adolescent dietitian at a large hospital for almost 10 years.

Acknowledgments

I would like to thank my many friends for their ideas and contributions that helped make this book possible. In addition, I would like to thank my children, Heather and Corey, and husband, Andy, for their support and help in taste-tasting the recipes.

                                                    Sandy Nissenberg

I would like to thank my friends for their support, ideas, and encouragement while writing this book. Thanks also to my husband, Stuart, and to my children, Lisa, Jeff, and Michael, for recipe suggestions and their willingness to participate in taste-testing.

                                                    Barb Pearl

The authors would also like to thank the faculty and children at Prairie and Willow Grove Elementary Schools in Buffalo Grove, Illinois, for sharing lunch and creative suggestions with us.

And special thanks to Natalie Fox and Einav Zahar, for their art on the front and back covers, respectively.

Table of Contents

Introduction

You spend your child's early years introducing new foods and teaching the importance of a well-balanced diet. You might feel like you have just gotten this under control when your child heads off to first grade and forgets everything you taught him about eating right. Once your child starts spending more time each day with friends than he does with you, he seem.s. to change his tune on what he likes and dislikes. Peer pressure and socially accepted foods begin to take priority. You have to find a way to accept that at this point in life you are beginning to lose control over your child's food preferences.

Your child wants the same lunch every day. Mornings are stressful as you prepare yourself for a day's work and pack lunches at the same time. You find that you are low on supplies and have no clue what to put in the lunch box. You feel like there is never any variety for lunch. We are all in this together.

Brown Bag Success is written for parents, like us, like you, of school-aged kids who want to get the most out of their child's lunch-box meals. We bring you the latest information about what to pack, how to pack, what to pack in, and what's in the foods you pack.

This book shares many lunch-box ideas, along with comments and suggestions from professionals, parents, and kids on what works, what doesn't, and how you can make your lunch-making life easier. We included a cycle menu and a variety of recipes that might work well with your schedule and can be enjoyed by the entire family. Nutrient analyses included with the recipes might also help you plan for your child's (and family's) needs.

Preparing and packing lunch-box meals can be stressful. We have tried to make it a little easier for you to handle. But it is only one meal of the day. It is still up to you to offer other nutritious meals and snacks during the rest of the day that complement the lunch. The habits and food choices and children develop now will last a lifetime. You can make the difference.

Happy, healthy eating for you and your family.

Sandra K. Nissenberg, M.S., R.D.
Barbara N. Pearl, M.S., R.D.

Your Guide to Packing Healthy Lunches

It's that time again. Time to pack another lunch. Another peanut butter and jelly sandwich (maybe chips and cookies, too). Are there any other options besides these?

That's what we all seem to experience day in and day out. It seems as though it's always time to pack that bag and, of course, the same thing always goes in it.

Read on...

As parents, we get tired of packing the same lunch every day, even though that's what our kids want. Do we try to get them to try new foods or let them have the same lunch day after day, week after week, month after month, and year after year? How can we get our kids to experience new choices? If we try something new, will it be eaten, traded, or thrown out?

How can we give our kids a healthy meal without adding stress to our own lives? What are some quick new foods my children would like and ones I'll feel good about packing?

Even the most carefully thought out lunch can be thrown out or traded away at school. If your child is mocked because his lunch is different from what the other kids have, he won't want to eat it in front of his friends. He wants to be happy with his lunch—no surprises (unless they're good ones!). You need to ask your child what he wants and what he doesn't want and continue to note what gets eaten, traded, or discarded. Being tuned in to your child's preferences makes you a partner rather than a rival. It helps keep communication open, which is a step in the right direction as your child grows.

Keep your kids involved. Let them have choices, and encourage them to help as much as possible with preparation and packing. The more they do, the more they'll eat and the more responsible they'll become. It's a win-win situation.

Keep reading...

We'll give you a quick course on nutrition, tips to reduce stressful mornings, ways to incorporate new foods, information about packing and storing foods, ideas for making lunchtime fun, responses to common concerns of parents, views from kids on what they like and what they don't, actual cycle menu plans, lots of fun new recipes, and much more.

10 Smart Tips for Packing the Lunch Box

1. Seek Wise Choices

A healthy, well-balanced lunch should be built like the food pyramid (see next page). Begin with a selection from as many food groups as you can. Lunch should include a high-protein food, fresh fruit or vegetable, bread or starch, a treat, and finally juice, water, or milk. Vary the choices daily to bring variety into lunch. Even if your child is stuck on the same sandwich every day, change the foods that go along with it.

Add color, texture, and flavors. Kids like variety in colors, textures, and flavors. For example, the color combination of a turkey sandwich on white bread with vanilla wafers might not be as appealing as a chicken drumstick, baby carrots, and mini chocolate-chip muffin. Colorful foods are more appealing and more appetizing. Try red, green, yellow, orange, and purple foods. You'll want to pack foods with different textures as well. Plan for both crunchy and smooth textures for contrast. A crunchy peanut butter sandwich with chips and a fresh apple might keep your child munching his entire lunch period. And a child who's missing a few teeth might not even get halfway through this lunch. You'll also want to consider the flavors of foods. Include several different flavors in each lunch, contrasting strong with mild flavors. But be wary of strong-flavored foods that may smell after sitting in a lunch bag for several hours. You don't want your child's entire backpack or math book smelling like dill pickles.

And don't forget to consider your child's likes and dislikes. Within each food group you have a variety of food choices. Every few months, ask your child to help you create a list of foods he would like for lunch and those he would not. Even though he may eat certain foods at home, don't always assume these will be well accepted at school, too. If a certain food isn't "socially acceptable" it won't be one your child will want to pull out of his lunch bag. Foods are commonly thrown out or traded during the lunch hour. Check with your child daily and ask him what he liked about lunch and what he didn't. By being in tune with your child's preferences, you'll make everyone happier.

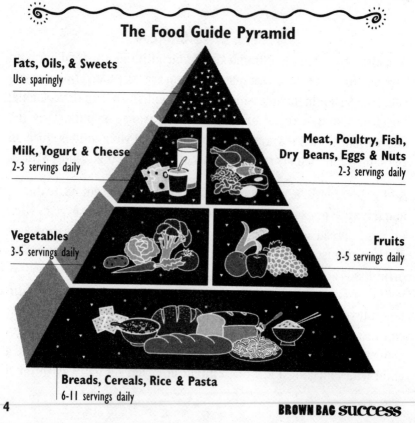

The Food Guide Pyramid

Fats, Oils, & Sweets
Use sparingly

Milk, Yogurt & Cheese
2-3 servings daily

Meat, Poultry, Fish, Dry Beans, Eggs & Nuts
2-3 servings daily

Vegetables
3-5 servings daily

Fruits
3-5 servings daily

Breads, Cereals, Rice & Pasta
6-11 servings daily

2. Plan Ahead

We always have good intentions, but when we get down to the last minute, we might not have what we need or want for lunch. Just as it's a good idea to plan weekly menus for dinner, it's also wise to consider weekly lunch-box meals.

Here are some ideas that can save you time and energy:

Keep a pad of paper available for the kids, or for yourself, to jot down any foods you want or need to purchase at the grocery store.

Use our Brown Bag Success Monthly Cycle Menu or create a cycle menu of your own. This can help tremendously when shopping and packing lunches.

Take your kids with you to the grocery store and ask them for suggestions of foods they would like in their lunch.

Prepare muffins, quick breads, cookies, trail mixes, granola bars, soups, chicken drumsticks, and other items on weekends when you may have more time, and keep them handy in the refrigerator for daily packing. You can also prepackage some items in bags or containers for easy stuffing.

Use your freezer. You can prepack and freeze single servings of many types of foods. When you find yourself in a pinch or just can't get to the store, consult your freezer supply. Keep in mind that some foods freeze better than others. Sliced meat, chicken, hard boiled egg yolks, quiche, shredded cheese, fruit juice, peanut butter, chili, bread, and cream cheese all freeze well. Foods that don't freeze as well include hard boiled egg whites, cottage cheese, raw vegetables, mayonnaise, jam, and pickles.

3. Stock Your Pantry and Refrigerator

It's frustrating to discover you're out of peanut butter just when it's time to pack lunches, especially when your child won't eat anything else. Don't wait for this to happen. Keeping a well stocked pantry and refrigerator is a good habit to get into both for meals prepared at home and for those packed for school.

You might want to keep your pantry and refrigerator stocked with these lunch-box food suggestions:

Bread (white, whole wheat, raisin, tortillas, bagels, pita)
Pasta (in a variety of shapes and sizes)
Tuna (packed in water)
Peanut butter (smooth and chunky)
Jam, fruit spread
Canned fruit (mandarin oranges, pineapple, fruit cocktail, peaches, pears)
Canned rolls, breadsticks
Fresh fruit (apples, bananas, oranges, grapes, pears)
Fresh vegetables (carrots, celery, cucumbers, sweet peppers, cherry tomatoes)
Dried fruit (raisins, apricots, apples, pineapple)
Granola, granola bars
Trail mix
Dry cereal
Cheese (all types, slices, cubes, shredded, sticks)
Fruit juice (individual containers of 100% juice)
Pudding, jello, applesauce, fruit mixes (individual containers)
Pretzels, crackers, graham crackers, popcorn, peanuts, sunflower seeds
Cookies (vanilla wafers, fig bars, animal crackers)

And don't forget the wraps:

plastic margarine or yogurt containers, plastic cups with lids
plastic sandwich containers
plastic wrap
twist ties
individual plastic bags
resealable plastic bags
foil
paper lunch bags
napkins or character napkins
plastic utensils
wide-mouth thermos

4. Use Leftovers

Using leftovers for lunch can provide a delicious, nutritious meal at school as well as being a great timesaver for you. Plan on it.

When preparing dinner, especially on the weekend when there is more time available, make a serving or two extra. Chicken, pizza, pasta salad, soup, tossed salad, fresh cut up vegetables, muffins, banana bread, cookies, and more can all be made ahead, prepackaged, and added to lunch on a regular basis.

Pack these food items in plastic bags or reusable plastic containers and put them in a special section of the refrigerator. Be sure to label each item, so you know what's inside. Then select from those leftovers when packing your child's lunch. It couldn't be easier.

We have included many recipes in this book for foods that can be used as dinner meals as well as for lunches. Select the ones you and your kids like and begin enjoying more foods and saving yourself some time and frustration along the way.

5. Pack the Night Before

There's nothing more stressful than trying to do too much in the morning before getting the kids off to school. The kids need breakfast, you discover additional homework to be done, the phone rings and on top of it all, you haven't even begun to pack lunches. If you pack those lunches at night, it will make a big difference in your stress level, and you'll probably end up packing healthier lunches, too.

Each night after dinner set out the lunch boxes, plastic containers, napkins, utensils, and milk money. Think about any dinner leftovers you might be able to add to the lunch. Then while you are cleaning up the dishes, plan tomorrow's lunch for the kids, and yourself too. Wrap up an extra chicken leg. Drop a few leftover side dishes or a dinner roll into a plastic bag or plastic container. Sandwiches can also be made. Fruits and vegetables can be cut up. Muffins, cakes, and cookies can be wrapped. The entire lunch can be put in the lunch box and stored overnight in the refrigerator.

To make your life even easier, refer to our Brown Bag Success Monthly Cycle Menu starting on page 20. If you have a well-stocked pantry and refrigerator, all you have to do is follow the menu plans— you'll never have to think about what to pack for lunch again.

6. Be Creative

In today's busy world, a little creativity and some preplanning can make lunch easy to prepare, fun to eat, and healthy, too! Try these ideas when packing lunches to go. Enjoy!

- Use cookie cutters to cut your bread in different shapes for sandwiches. These can be especially fun around holiday time. Hearts, stars, bears, boats, butterflies, and more can bring a lunchtime smile.

- Use a large glass to cut circles out of bread. Add peanut butter, cream cheese, tuna salad, etc. Pop in pretzel sticks for legs and raisins as eyes to make a spider sandwich.

- Make fruit, vegetable, cheese, or meat kabobs instead of sandwiches.

- Try different types and shapes of bread. Have you tried whole wheat, rye, pumpernickel, potato, raisin, oatmeal, French, or cheese breads? How about sending a sandwich on a sub or kaiser roll, a hamburger or hot dog bun, a bagel, rice cakes, or graham crackers? Or how about a sandwich in a pita or rolled up in a tortilla?

- Add color and crunch to lunch with raw vegetables and fruit. Carrots, for example, can be left whole, grated, or cut into many shapes—sticks or circles. Lowfat dips add some dipping fun. Apples and grapes come in many varieties. Try them all!

- Add a twist to an old sandwich favorite. Instead of jelly with peanut butter, try honey, marshmallow fluff, bananas, raisins, or granola.

- Change the accompaniments. Instead of chips, send popcorn (regular or flavored with Parmesan cheese or spices), pretzels (vary the shape), dry cereal, or homemade sweet potato chips. Vary the desserts and beverages, too.

- Try adding a variety of nutritious and thirst-quenching drinks to lunch. Suggestions include lowfat or skim milk (flavored or plain),

100% fruit juices, or bottled water. If you like, pack chocolate or strawberry powder in the lunch box and your child can just drop it into the milk carton, and stir or shake.

Instead of a sandwich, send cheese and crackers (or breadsticks or rice cakes), breadstick roll-ups (turkey, roast beef, ham, or cheese wrapped around a breadstick), strips of meat and/or cheese with raw vegetables and crackers, cold pasta with cheese, raw or cooked vegetables, leftovers from last night's dinner, or cold pizza.

A variety of desserts can also perk up a lunch. Include cookies, muffins, and cupcakes your child enjoys. If you can bake and freeze a large amount ahead of time (in a "spare" moment), you can make desserts healthier by reducing the amount of sugar and fat in the recipe.

7. Go Small: Enough Is Enough

Parents often wonder how much to pack for lunch. Adult size servings can overwhelm a child, causing disinterest in the entire meal. Providing a balanced meal with variety and the right serving sizes helps with meal acceptance. Don't worry! A healthy child that is growing is getting enough to eat. If your child is hungry, he will ask for more.

Besides having a child-sized appetite, the lunch period at most schools is short. By the time a child finds a seat, talks to his friends, and finally pulls out his lunch, there may be less than 15 minutes to eat. Most of a large lunch will probably get thrown out.

Children enjoy small amounts of a variety of foods. It's like opening presents at a birthday. So, if you provide a main dish that contains some protein (a sandwich), one or two side dishes (pretzels and a fruit), a dessert (2 cookies), and a drink (milk), that will be plenty to eat. There is a chart that outlines child-sized portions on the next page.

Suggested Serving Sizes for Kids

	4-6 Years	7-10 Years
Breads and Grains		
bread	1 slice	1 slice
pasta, rice	1/3-1/2 cup	1/2-3/4 cup
pretzels	3/4 ounce	1 ounce
crackers	5-7	5-7
bagel, bun	1/2	1/2
Vegetables		
cooked or raw	1/3 cup	1/2 cup
Fruits		
fresh	1/2-1 small	1 medium
juice	1/2 cup	3/4 cup
canned	1/3 cup	1/2 cup
Milk/Dairy Products		
milk	3/4 cup	1 cup
cheese	1 ounce	1 1/2 ounces
yogurt	3/4 cup	1 cup
Lean Meat/Poultry/Fish/Dry Beans/Nuts & Eggs		
meat/poultry/fish	1 1/2 ounces	2-3 ounces
dry beans, cooked	1/2 cup	1/2-1 cup
peanut butter	1-2 tablespoons	2-3 tablespoons
eggs	1	1-2

8. Pack it Right and Be Kind to the Environment

Technology has made it easier than ever to pack lunches while being environmentally aware. A wide variety of lunch bags are available, as well as environmentally-friendly products to wrap food and carry beverages. Wash and reuse these containers as much as possible.

Bags and Boxes Waterproof, insulated nylon bags in which food can stay cool for hours are available on the market. The tops fold down and stay secure with Velcro. Most of them are machine washable. Some come with their own lunch kits or plastic containers so sandwiches and side dishes stay fresh and in one piece. These kits can be purchased separately also.

The old-fashioned lunch box is still available today. Most of them are made of durable plastic and contain thermal containers that can withstand the abuse young children put them through. Lunch boxes are also available in soft-sided, insulated nylon in a variety of colors and designs. The thermos and lunch box/bag can be bought separately. This may be a good idea if you pack a lot of soups and beverages, mainly because you can buy a better quality thermos this way.

A variety of bags to tote lunches are available in grocery stores, drug and hardware stores, and discount stores. You'll find the best supply in the summer, right before school starts. But most stores carry them year-round. Remember that the "cool" design this year may be "out" next year. If you choose a bag for more than one year, try to be practical in your selection.

Let's not forget the old brown bag. If temperature is not a problem or rigid packaging is not necessary to protect food, then your basic brown bag is fine. Have a contest to see how many uses you can get out of one brown bag. The kids will love it! They're recyclable, inexpensive, and readily available in most grocery and discount stores.

The Inside Story The easiest wrap for most sandwiches and side dishes is the plastic sandwich bag that either zips closed or folds over so food cannot slide out. There are many sizes of these bags, making them versatile in what they can hold. Plastic wrap can also be used for a variety of foods. Many schools have separate containers for recycling plastic wraps.

Rigid plastic reusable containers designed for specific uses are also available. There are single containers with dividers that hold many items and individual containers that hold single servings. Many shapes and sizes are available. Since these are washable and reusable, they are a terrific choice to keep our environment waste-free. But, the problem is having your child remember to bring them home. Some children might be better off using a previously-used plastic food or margarine container that has been thoroughly cleaned. This way, if it is thrown out, it won't be a great loss.

A word of caution: Don't use any container that was not meant to be used with food. Toxic fumes could transfer to the food or melt into the food if heated. Also, never assume a container can be reused. Some packages may pass bacteria or draw insects to food. If you're not sure if a container can be reused, don't use it. Don't take a chance with food.

9. Get Kids Involved

Make the lunch you pack more tempting by letting the kids help. Try these suggestions:

- Take your child with you when you shop for food. If schedules don't allow you to shop together, have your child make you a list of items to buy at the store.

- Give your child a choice on lunch options. If he feels you are involving him in these decisions, he may feel more like eating lunch.

- Let your child prepare or at least help pack his lunch. When he makes his own sandwich, for example, it gives him a feeling of independence and responsibility. He will be more likely to eat the lunch he helped create.

- Have your child pick out a new recipe or food to try. He can then help prepare it and pack it for lunch.

- It's OK to occasionally pack an item you consider unhealthy, but your child enjoys very much. If you combine this item with healthy choices, you can still balance the lunch and let your child have some say in it as well.

- Keep communication lines open. Ask your kids regularly what they enjoyed in their lunch, what they didn't enjoy, if any foods were thrown out and why, and how you can make lunch better.

10. Add a Personal Touch to Lunch

Kids love fast food meals, mostly because of the toy or prize they get with it. Try making a prize of your own or try some of our other ideas for personalizing your child's lunch.

- Save small toys from cereal boxes or buy small inexpensive toys or trinkets (shoelaces, erasers, crayons, bookmarks, personalized pencils, etc.) and include them with lunch. Surprise!

- Include a sticker, riddle, poem, joke, special note, or invitation to an upcoming family event. It'll bring a smile at lunchtime.

- Why not drop a baseball or basketball trading card in with lunch? It's fun to collect them.

- Include a countdown reminder to an upcoming party or vacation. "Only 2 more days 'til your birthday."

- Send a game for recess like jacks, Chinese jumprope, a small deck of cards, or a do-it-yourself puzzle. Cut up a postcard or picture and have your child reassemble it.

- Make up a reason for a celebration, like an "unbirthday party" or the first day of spring. Include something special for the occasion.

- Send a special treat, labeled, "Share with a Friend."

- Pack a secret message in a made-up code and see if your child can figure it out.

- Send a "word-of-the-day." Your child will increase his vocabulary without even trying.

- Pack a character napkin (they're not just for birthday parties). They add pizzazz to lunch.

- Use decorative plastic bags, colored paper bags, and fun lunch containers. Try decorating a lunch bag with stickers, markers, or paints. Lunch always tastes better if it's in a fun package.

Answers

to the Most Commonly Asked
Questions from Concerned Parents

1. How can I bring variety into my child's lunch?

You do not necessarily have to change the type of sandwich to add variety to your child's lunch. If you change the side dishes (type of drink, vegetables, fruit, chips/pretzels, etc.) and the type of bread that is on the sandwich (wheat, rye, pita, crackers, bun, bagel, etc.), then you can add variety also. Remember—no surprises! Communicating with your child about what's for lunch is important.

2. What is there beyond peanut butter sandwiches?

By reviewing our Brown Bag Success Monthly Cycle Menu (page 20), you can see there *is* life beyond peanut butter sandwiches. If your child is not ready to try a new type of sandwich filling, then maybe packing peanut butter in different ways will be your option. Try putting peanut butter on graham crackers or on celery or an apple. Try various types of breads or different combinations with the peanut butter, like mashed bananas, applesauce, or shredded carrots. Have you discussed having breakfast for lunch? Send cereal or cold French toast and syrup with fruit and have your child buy milk at school. Sending soup in a thermos is another option, especially on cold winter days.

Don't fight with your child over peanut butter! You'll always lose. Peanut butter, especially the lower-fat version, is basically a healthy food. When your child is ready, he'll choose a new sandwich filling. Keep offering different options to try at home, set a good eating example yourself, and keep talking with your child.

3. What are some good sandwich alternatives?

Instead of sandwiches, try meat and/or cheese kabobs or wrap the meat or cheese around a pretzel rod or breadstick. Having breakfast for lunch (see above) is a fun change. Soup or chili in a thermos is another idea. Add a bagel or crackers and juice to drink and you have a balanced lunch. And don't forget about leftover pizza, macaroni and cheese, pasta, or Chinese food. Kids love them!

4. My child does not drink milk.
How can I add calcium to his diet?

The best way to provide calcium is through foods from the dairy group—yogurt, milk, cheese, cottage cheese, pudding, etc. Although not as good of a source, some vegetables provide calcium too—broccoli, cabbage, artichokes, snap beans, carrots, soybeans. Some children will tolerate milk if it is hidden in a food, such as hot or cold cereals, flavored (chocolate/strawberry) milks, or cream soups. All these can be sent for lunch. There are also some juices on the market that have calcium added to them. The best solution is not to depend on only one source, but to eat a variety of calcium-containing foods every day.

5. How can I prevent my child from trading
or throwing out his lunch?

Even the best planned, most creative lunches will sometimes be traded or thrown out. There are some factors parents cannot control, such as peer pressure, time limitations for the lunch period, and a child's emotions. But, if you communicate about what's wanted for lunch and if your child participates in making the lunch, the chances of that lunch being discarded or given away are much less.

6. Should I be concerned about the fat content of my child's lunch?

The recommended amount of fat in a child's diet is 30 percent of their daily caloric needs. Most children do not need to count grams of fat in their diet. By limiting fried and fatty foods and following simple healthy eating guidelines outlined in the food pyramid, in addition to being physically active, most children can eat a balanced diet and maintain a healthy weight.

If a child is overweight or putting on excess weight, then it may be wise to take a closer look at his food intake and activity level. In general, if children frequently eat out (three or four times per week) or if they frequently snack and remain inactive, they can be susceptible to gaining excess weight. Unfortunately, we are seeing this happen more often in our fast-paced society as we depend on restaurants and convenience foods more and more. If this is your situation, then choosing lower-fat foods at your favorite restaurant would be advisable, as well as balancing higher-fat meals with lower-fat options at meals served at home and at school. Also, remember to incorporate physical activity whenever possible.

Monthly Cycle Menu

Schools usually send home a monthly cycle menu outlining the hot lunches (if available) served each day. This list is helpful when deciding whether to buy or bring your lunch that particular day. We have made your lunch packing just as easy for you by creating our own Brown Bag Success Monthly Cycle Menu. Here we have combined recipes from this book (*) with staples and family favorites to help you figure out what to include in those lunches. You can use our ideas or create some of your own.

Week 1

Monday
Peanut Butter Surprise*
Pretzel Rods
Dried Apples*
Milk

Tuesday
Turkey Club Sandwich*
Baby Carrot Sticks with Dip
Vanishing Oatmeal Chipsters*
Juice

Wednesday
Inside-Out Cheese Sandwich*
Sweet Coleslaw*
Fig Bars
Chocolate Milk

Thursday
Orange Peanut Butter Sandwich*
Fresh Fruit on a Stick*
Chocolate Graham Cracker
Milk

Friday
Pasta with Artichokes and Cheese*
Breadstick
Fresh Apple
Milk

Week 2

Monday
Easy Chili*
Sweet Corn-Bread Muffin*
Grapes
Juice

Tuesday
Crunchy-Chewy Peanut Butter
and Jelly Sandwich*
Tortilla Chips*
Pudding
Milk

Wednesday
Chicken Fajita Pita*
Oriental Nut Mix*
Banana
Juice

Thursday
Tortellini with Parmesan Cheese*
Pretzel Rod
Yogurt Raisins
Chocolate Milk

Friday
Turkey Roll*
Parmesan Popcorn*
Mandarin Oranges
Milk

Week 3

Monday
Geez-O-Cheez Kabobs*
Zucchini Bread*
Chocolate Milk

Tuesday
Chicken Soup to Go*
Mini Bagel
Waldorf Salad*
Juice

Wednesday
Graham Cracker Peanut Butter and
Banana Sandwich*
Homemade Potato Chips*
Raisins
Milk

Thursday
Lunch on a Stick*
Peanut Butter and Jam Muffin*
Juice

Friday
Tuna-Apple Sandwich*
Celery Sticks
Vanilla Wafers
Milk

Week 4

Monday
ABC Veggie Soup*
One Bowl Banana Bread*
String Cheese
Chocolate Milk

Tuesday
Mini Drumsticks*
Cucumber Slices
Granola Bar
Juice

Wednesday
Fine French Toast*
Fruit Salad Medley*
Milk

Thursday
Mini Meat Loaf Sandwich*
Fresh Pepper Chunks
Applesauce Cup
Juice

Friday
Open-Faced Sunshine Sandwich*
Apple Fruit Leather*
Milk

Tips and Tricks

Make Your Own Kid's Meal

Kids love fast food kid's meals. Try making one of your own:

- Save small toys from cereal boxes or purchase some small, inexpensive toys or stickers and drop them in with lunch. What a nice treat!

- Include a different baseball or collectable card with each lunch, and let your child save them up. It's fun to save these up from week to week.

- Recycle old toys from kid's meals. After a few years, kids forget about certain toys. They can bring a smile and some fun to lunch.

Add a Personal Touch to Your Child's Lunch

- Let your kids make their own lunch containers. Paint or color canvas bags, plastic totes, or thermos containers found at craft stores.

- Use a variety of cookie cutters to cut bread for sandwiches or to make cheese cut-outs.

Jot down messages, jokes, riddles, poems, or special messages. Put them in small envelopes and add to lunch.

Pack It Right. Pack It Tight.

Your child's favorite foods won't be favorites any more if they look unappealing by lunchtime. Smashed, squishy, out-of-shape sandwiches, broken chips and cookies, and wet raw vegetables will likely end up in the trash. When packing your portable lunches keep these ideas in mind:

Keep needed supplies on hand for quick and easy packing. Plastic wrap, foil, twist ties, sandwich bags, napkins, and plastic utensils are important staples.

Buy your child a good wide-mouthed thermos if he carries soups or beverages. Check the thermos carefully for leakage and insulation.

Keep old plastic margarine containers for canned and cut-up fruits and vegetables, cheese cubes, frozen items, or other small foods you want separated and stored tightly. These containers are also good to use for waste-free, environmentally-friendly lunches.

Keep Lunches Cool...and Cool...

Lunch boxes and insulated bags keep in the cold better than plain paper bags. If you want to be sure to keep your lunch cool, especially if refrigeration is not available, try these "cool" suggestions your child won't frown on.

Drop a frozen juice box into a lunch container. It keeps food cool and is ready to drink at lunchtime.

Freeze water in an old margarine container or plastic water bottle and place in the lunch box.

Make sandwiches on frozen bread. The coolness from the bread helps keep the rest of the lunch cool. Bread will be thawed by lunchtime.

Freeze grapes or banana slices and add to the lunch box.

- Try mini ice packs or freezer gel packs that can be frozen and inserted with lunch.

- For meals that require extra coolness, be sure to purchase insulated and tightly sealed containers.

- Be sure to clean the lunch box container daily. Wash it with warm soapy water and let it air-dry.

Handling Food Jags

Food jags, or eating one food to the exclusion of almost all others, is quite common among preschool and school-aged children. It's no cause for alarm. In fact, it's probably best to pay as little attention as possible to the food jag.

Nutritional deficiencies develop over long periods of time. Most food jags last a few weeks. Hopefully, with time, your child will get bored with the particular food and try other foods. Remember, it's not so important what a child eats over a few days, but rather over the long haul. Meanwhile, you'll probably need to continue packing your child's favorite food, but also provide a variety of other choices.

If you find yourself tackling a food jag, try these helpful tips on moving out of it:

- Settle on one food item that you will continually pack in the lunch box. Alternate the other choices.

- If it's peanut butter and jelly you despise so much, try offering other combinations with the peanut butter or change the bread you serve with it.

- Offer other choices and a variety of foods at home to help balance out your child's intake.

- Let your child help prepare meals and snacks, thereby creating a greater interest in the foods.

- Set a good example of healthy eating by eating a variety of foods yourself.

Don't draw attention to the eating jag; ignore it.

Be patient with your child when he tries a new food. Don't take it personally if your child rejects it. Try again later. When your child is very hungry, he may be more likely to accept it.

Keep in mind that many food jags are centered around peanut butter, cheese, macaroni, pizza, dry cereal, and chocolate milk. All of these foods are healthy choices for kids. Don't be overly concerned.

Try Breakfast for Lunch

Kids get a kick out of eating breakfast for lunch every now and then. Make it a weekly routine or a special surprise. Have you ever thought about...

packing small boxes of dry cereal? Just pour on the carton of milk and it's ready to eat. (Don't forget the spoon.)

French toast or French toast sticks?

pancakes or waffles? (Send syrup for dipping.)

hard-cooked eggs?

bagel and cream cheese sandwiches?

The Recipes

The recipes included here are just a sample of the types of foods you can include in your child's lunch box. Try your own variations of many of them and be creative.

The nutrient analysis is provided by the Food Processor II Nutritional Analysis Software. Calories, protein, carbohydrates, fat, and food exchange information is indicated. Figures are rounded to the closest whole number. When several choices are provided, the first food is included in the analysis. Optional ingredients are not analyzed.

The information included in the analyses can help you as you plan for the other meals of the day. If you include higher-fat foods at one meal, you may wish to balance foods out by including lower-fat foods at another. You can see from the exchanges listed how a particular recipe fits into the overall diet. You should include food groups not eaten at lunch during other meals and snacks of the day in order to meet your child's nutrient needs.

We have included a snowflake on those recipes that require refrigeration or an ice pack to keep them cold. If you do not have the appropriate container or ice pack for your child's lunch, or if it is an extremely hot day, do not choose these items.

Simple Soups

Soup Mix-Ups

ABC Veggie Soup

Chicken Soup to Go

Easy Chili

Cheesy-Tomato Soup

Corn Chowder

Very Veggie Soup

Chilly Cherry Fruit Soup

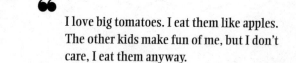

I love big tomatoes. I eat them like apples.
The other kids make fun of me, but I don't
care, I eat them anyway.

Becca Bryan, age 10

Soup Mix-Ups

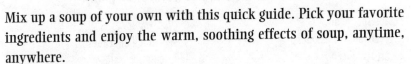

Mix up a soup of your own with this quick guide. Pick your favorite ingredients and enjoy the warm, soothing effects of soup, anytime, anywhere.

Start with a soup base, and add some protein, veggies, pasta, and toppings for an out-of-this-world creation.

Soup Base	Protein	Vegetables	Pasta/Grains	Toppings
chicken broth	chicken	tomatoes	rice	croutons
beef broth	turkey	carrots	couscous	sunflower seeds
vegetable broth	beef	peas	noodles	shredded cheese
oriental broth	shrimp	mixed veggies	tortellini	tortilla chips
bouillon cube	canned beans	corn	macaroni	
consommé	chickpeas	celery	spaghetti	
		onion	alphabet noodles	
		mushrooms	barley	

ABC Veggie Soup

Kids enjoy the alphabet noodles in this soup so much, they forget they are eating vegetables too. It's a great option for a cold, snowy day.

1 tablespoon oil
3 green onions, chopped
2 carrots, sliced
2 stalks celery, sliced
15-ounce can stewed tomatoes

4 cups water
4 beef bouillon cubes
1/2 teaspoon salt
1/4 teaspoon pepper
1/2 cup alphabet noodles, uncooked

Heat oil in large saucepan over medium heat. Add onions, carrots, and celery. Cook until vegetables are tender, about 10 minutes. Add tomatoes, water, bouillon cubes, salt, pepper, and noodles. Bring mixture to a boil. Reduce heat, cover, and simmer for 30 minutes, stirring occasionally. If making in advance, heat 1 cup of the soup in the microwave before packing in thermos.

Servings: 6
Calories: 78 • Protein: 2 grams • Carbohydrates: 13 grams • Fat: 3 grams
Exchanges: 1/2 bread, 1 vegetable, 1/2 fat

Chicken Soup to Go

Here's a real comfort food. It will make you feel good all over.

2 14 1/2-ounce cans chicken broth
1 cooked chicken breast, shredded
3 carrots, peeled and chopped

3 stalks celery, chopped
2 onions, chopped
1/2 teaspoon pepper

Combine broth and chicken in large saucepan. Add remaining ingredients. Bring to boil. Reduce heat and simmer 15 minutes or until vegetables are tender. Reheat soup in microwave before packing in thermos.

Servings: 6
Calories: 83 • Protein: 8 grams • Carbohydrates: 7 grams • Fat: 2 grams
Exchanges: 1/2 meat, 1 vegetable

Easy Chili

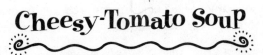

Try this easy chili in a thermos. With tortilla chips and fresh fruit on the side, your lunch is complete.

1/4 cup chopped onions
1 pound ground beef
  (or try ground turkey)
15-ounce can diced tomatoes

15-ounce can kidney beans
1 teaspoon chili powder
1 1/2 cups water

In large saucepan, combine onions and beef (or turkey) over medium heat. Brown beef, then drain excess fat. Add remaining ingredients to saucepan. Cook until mixture boils, stirring frequently. Reduce heat to a simmer and cook an additional 10 minutes. If making in advance, heat 1 cup of the chili mixture in the microwave before packing in thermos.

Servings: 6
Calories: 241 • Protein: 17 grams • Carbohydrates: 15 grams • Fat: 12 grams
Exchanges: 1/2 bread, 2 meat, 1/2 vegetable, 1 1/2 fat

Cheesy-Tomato Soup

**Tomato soup can hit the spot on a cold day.
Jazz it up with some shredded cheese. You'll love it.**

10 3/4-ounce can tomato soup
1 soup can lowfat milk

1/4 teaspoon Worcestershire sauce
3/4 cup shredded cheddar cheese

Combine soup and milk in medium saucepan. Bring soup to boil, stirring constantly. Add Worcestershire sauce. Reduce heat to low. Add cheese. Stir until cheese melts. If making in advance, heat 1 cup of the soup in the microwave before packing in thermos.

Servings: 6
Calories: 116 • Protein: 6 grams • Carbohydrates: 9 grams • Fat: 6 grams
Exchanges: 1/2 meat, 1/2 vegetable, 1 fat

Corn Chowder

**This soup is so easy to make and so delicious.
Why not make it for your kids today?**

1 tablespoon margarine	2 cups lowfat milk
2 potatoes, peeled and cubed	1/2 teaspoon salt
1 cup frozen corn niblets	1/4 teaspoon pepper

In large saucepan, heat margarine over medium heat. Add potatoes.
Cook until potatoes are tender. Add corn, milk, salt, and pepper. Heat
until hot, but do not boil.

Servings: 4
Calories: 178 • Protein: 6 grams • Carbohydrates: 28 grams • Fat: 5 grams
Exchanges: 1 bread, 1/2 milk, 1/2 fat

Very Veggie Soup

**Vegetable soups are so hearty and nutritious. This easy-to-make
recipe has so many variations. You can add any leftover frozen
vegetables. You can also add any type of pasta or rice.**

2 14 1/2-ounce cans vegetable broth	1/4 teaspoon oregano
10-ounce package frozen vegetables	1/4 teaspoon thyme
1/4 teaspoon basil	1/2 cup pasta or rice, uncooked

In large saucepan, combine all ingredients except pasta or rice. Heat
to boiling. Lower heat to simmer. Add pasta. Simmer an additional 10
minutes.

Servings: 6
Calories: 99 • Protein: 6 grams • Carbohydrates: 17 grams • Fat: 1 gram
Exchanges: 1/2 bread, 1 vegetable

Chilly Cherry Fruit Soup

When it's hot and sticky outside and you want
something refreshing to cool you off, this soup is great!
What a delicious way to get the kids to eat their fruit.
Pack it in a thermos or plastic container.

16-ounce can cherry pie filling
2 cups water
1 cinnamon stick
1/3 cup blueberries

6 strawberries, sliced
6 grapes, sliced
1/4 cup sour cream, optional

In large saucepan, combine pie filling, water, and cinnamon stick.
Bring to boil. Partially cover and simmer for 10 minutes. Remove
from heat. Cool. Chill soup in refrigerator until ready to serve. Add
other fruits or serve plain. Top with sour cream if desired.

Servings: 4
Calories: 142 • Protein: 1 gram • Carbohydrates: 34 grams • Fat: 1 gram
Exchanges: 2 fruit

66 My mom takes little pieces of paper and
writes riddles and jokes on them. My
favorite joke in my lunch box one day was,
'Who is the smelliest fairy? Stinkerbell!'
We all laughed.

Claire Bullen, age 8 99

My mom puts character napkins in my
lunch. My favorite ones are Tweety Bird,
Sylvester, Taz, and Bugs Bunny.

Jaclyn Marzano, age 7

Sandwich Staples

Peanut Butter Mix-Ups

Peanut Butter Surprise

Crunchy-Chewy Peanut Butter
and Jelly Sandwich

Orange Peanut Butter
Sandwich

Apple-Cinnamon Sandwich

Chicken Fajita Pita

Graham Cracker Peanut Butter
and Banana Sandwich

Cinnamon/Cream Cheese
Roll Ups

Peanut Butter Pita

Inside-Out Cheese Sandwich

Open-Faced Sunshine Sandwich

Cheese Roll Surprise

Turkey Club Sandwich

Mini Meat Loaf Sandwich

Tuna-Apple Sandwich

Turkey Rolls

Garden Sandwich

> I usually throw away half of my sandwich—I don't tell my mom, she doesn't know, but it's just too much to eat.
>
> Natalie Fox, age 8

Peanut Butter Mix-Ups

It's amazing how creative you can get with the old peanut butter sandwich. Try to mix and match some of these combinations below.

Start with 2 tablespoons of peanut butter. Add 2 sides of bread, 1 tablespoon spread, and a touch of topping... and you've made the ultimate peanut butter sandwich.

Breads	Spreads	Toppings
white bread	jelly	raisins
whole wheat bread	honey	granola
raisin bread	maple syrup	chopped nuts
French bread	applesauce or chopped apples	sunflower seeds
pita pockets	mashed or sliced bananas	coconut
hot dog/hamburger bun	crushed pineapple	alfalfa sprouts
dinner roll	shredded carrots	dry cereal
mini bagel	shredded zucchini	
English muffin		
rice cake		
graham cracker		
party rye		

Servings: 1

Peanut Butter Surprise

You can make several of these easy sandwiches at a time and freeze the extras for up to a month. Then you will always have an extra sandwich made if you're squeezed for time.

6 slices sandwich bread,
  white or whole wheat
1/4 cup chunky peanut butter

2 tablespoons orange juice
1/4 cup raisins

Lay out bread slices. In small bowl, combine peanut butter and orange juice. Stir well. Add raisins. Spread filling between bread slices.

Servings: 3
Calories: 319 • Protein: 11 grams • Carbohydrates: 43 grams • Fat: 13 grams
Exchanges: 2 bread, 1/2 meat, 1 fruit, 1 1/2 fat

Crunchy-Chewy Peanut Butter and Jelly Sandwich

Here's a new twist to an old favorite.
Adding the granola and raisins to the peanut butter and jelly adds an additional nutritious boost.

2 slices sandwich bread,
  white or whole wheat
1 1/2 tablespoons peanut butter

1 teaspoon jelly or fruit spread
1 tablespoon prepared granola
1/2 tablespoon raisins

Lay out bread slices. Spread one slice of bread with peanut butter, then jelly. Sprinkle with granola and raisins. Top with other slice.

Servings: 1
Calories: 343 • Protein: 12 grams • Carbohydrates: 45 grams • Fat: 15 grams
Exchanges: 2 bread, 1 meat, 1 fruit, 2 fat

Orange Peanut Butter Sandwich

**This small variation to a peanut butter sandwich
can bring about a whole new favorite sandwich.**

2 slices bread, any type
1 tablespoon peanut butter

1 1/2 teaspoons orange juice
    concentrate

Lay out bread slices. Combine peanut butter with orange juice concentrate. Mix well. Spread on bread.

Servings: 1
Calories: 261 • Protein: 9 grams • Carbohydrates: 35 grams • Fat: 10 grams
Exchanges: 2 bread, 1/2 meat, 1/2 fruit, 1 fat

Apple-Cinnamon Sandwich

**Try this sweet, nutritious sandwich for
a change of pace. It's crunchy and delicious.**

4 slices sandwich or raisin bread
1/4 cup lowfat cream cheese
3 tablespoons chopped apple

2 tablespoons chopped walnuts
2 tablespoons chopped celery
1 teaspoon cinnamon

Lay out bread slices. Combine cream cheese, apple, walnuts, celery, and cinnamon. Mix well. Spread filling on two slices of bread. Top with other slices.

Servings: 2
Calories: 292 • Protein: 10 grams • Carbohydrates: 37 grams • Fat: 12 grams
Exchanges: 2 bread, 1/2 meat, 1 1/2 fat

Chicken Fajita Pita

Use last night's leftover chicken to make a fun lunch. While you're at it, you might just enjoy making one for yourself, too.

1/4 cup chopped cooked chicken
pinch of fajita seasoning mix
1/2 large or 1 small pita pocket

1/4 cup shredded lettuce
2 tablespoons shredded cheese,
  any type

Mix chicken with the pinch of fajita mix. Stuff chicken mixture into pita pocket. Add remaining ingredients.

Servings: 1
Calories: 207 • Protein: 16 grams • Carbohydrates: 17 grams • Fat: 8 grams
Exchanges: 1 bread, 1 1/2 meat, 1/2 fat

Graham Cracker Peanut Butter and Banana Sandwich

Graham crackers are a nice change and are fun to use for a finger sandwich. Of course, you can always put this mixture on bread, too.

4 graham crackers
2 tablespoons peanut butter

1/2 teaspoon cinnamon
1 small banana

Break graham crackers in half to make 2 squares. Spread each graham cracker with peanut butter. Sprinkle each with cinnamon. Arrange banana slices on peanut butter and cinnamon. Make sandwich with 2 graham cracker squares or eat open faced.

Servings: 2
Calories: 207 • Protein: 5 grams • Carbohydrates: 28 grams • Fat: 10 grams
Exchanges: 1/2 bread, 1/2 meat, 1 fruit, 1 fat

Cinnamon/Cream Cheese Roll-Ups

These bite-sized sandwiches make quite a hit at lunchtime. Kids love them for snacks, too.

4 slices soft sandwich bread,
   white or whole wheat
1/4 cup softened lowfat cream cheese
2 tablespoons raisins

2 tablespoons sugar
1 teaspoon cinnamon
2 tablespoons margarine

Preheat oven to 350°. Remove crusts from bread slices. Spread each slice of bread with cream cheese. Top with raisins. Roll each slice of bread into a log with cream cheese on the inside.

Mix sugar and cinnamon together in small bowl. Melt margarine in another bowl. Dip each roll (bread side, not ends) into margarine, then into sugar mixture. Cut each roll into 3 bite-sized pieces. Place on cookie sheet, seam side down. Bake roll-ups for 10 to 12 minutes or until light brown. Serve warm for a snack or cool as a lunch treat.

Servings: 4
Calories: 201 • Protein: 4 grams • Carbohydrates: 26 grams • Fat: 9 grams
Exchanges: 1 bread, 1/2 fruit, 1/2 fat

Peanut Butter Pita

Adding sprouts and carrots to your peanut butter sandwich adds crunch. Putting it all in a pita makes it fun to eat.

1 tablespoon peanut butter
1 teaspoon mayonnaise
2 tablespoons shredded carrots

1 teaspoon raisins
1/2 large or 1 small pita pocket
2 tablespoons alfalfa sprouts

Combine peanut butter with mayonnaise. Add carrots and raisins. Stuff mixture into pita pocket. Top with alfalfa sprouts.

Servings: 1
Calories: 226 • Protein: 7 grams • Carbohydrates: 24 grams • Fat: 12 grams
Exchanges: 1 bread, 1/2 meat, 1/2 fruit, 2 fat

Inside-Out Cheese Sandwich

Why does the bread always go on the outside?
You can try this recipe or make up some of your own inside-out
sandwiches with deli meats, turkey, or other cheeses.

1 slice sandwich bread
2 slices American cheese

1 teaspoon mayonnaise
or salad dressing

Flatten bread slice with rolling pin or with your hand. Spread bread with salad dressing or mayonnaise. Place cheese slices on top of bread, allowing about 1 1/2 inches of the cheese to hang over each side of the bread. Roll sandwich with cheese on the outside, bread on the inside.

Servings: 1
Calories: 248 • Protein: 11 grams • Carbohydrates: 18 grams • Fat: 15 grams
Exchanges: 1 bread, 1 meat, 1/2 milk, 2 fat

Open-Faced Sunshine Sandwich

You will need to pack this sandwich in a reusable
plastic container to keep it bright and sunny for lunch.
Of course, that means less waste, too.

1 slice bread, 1 rice cake, 1/2 English
muffin, or 1/2 hamburger bun
1 tablespoon peanut butter

8 tidbits canned pineapple (buy them
precut or cut one slice into 8 pieces)
1 teaspoon sunflower seeds

Spread peanut butter on bread of choice. Arrange pineapple tidbits in a circle, small edges to middle, to create the rays of the sun. Sprinkle sunflower seeds in center where all pieces of pineapple come together.

Servings: 1
Calories: 222 • Protein: 7 grams • Carbohydrates: 27 grams • Fat: 10 grams
Exchanges: 1 bread, 1/2 meat, 1 fruit, 1 1/2 fat

Cheese Roll Surprise

These sandwiches can make a quick dinner, with leftovers packed for lunch the next day. You can also add shredded chicken, turkey, tuna, or ham to the cheese mixture if desired.

1 package (10) refrigerated crescent rolls   Cooking spray
3/4 cup shredded cheese, any type

Preheat oven to 350°. Spray muffin tin with cooking spray. Open rolls and separate. Pat each roll down flat. Top each roll with a heaping tablespoon of cheese. Roll up jelly-roll style. Place rolls into muffin tins. Using pastry brush, brush rolls with small amount of water or milk. Bake 15 to 18 minutes or until browned.

Servings: 10
Calories: 149 • Protein: 4 grams • Carbohydrates: 13 grams • Fat: 9 grams
Exchanges: 1 bread, 1/2 meat, 1 1/2 fat

Turkey Club Sandwich

**This layered sandwich has many variations.
Try this one for a start, then see what else you can add.**

2 slices sandwich bread
1 teaspoon margarine or mayonnaise
1 slice thinly sliced deli turkey
1 slice crisp bacon, optional

1 slice tomato
1 lettuce leaf
1 slice cheese, any variety
2-3 pickle slices

Lightly toast bread. Spread bread with margarine. Arrange remaining ingredients on bread. Top with remaining slice of bread.

Servings: 1
Calories: 304 • Protein: 16 grams • Carbohydrates: 34 grams • Fat: 11 grams
Exchanges: 2 bread, 1 1/2 meat, 1 1/2 fat

Mini Meat Loaf Sandwich

**Kids like small items much better than larger ones.
Here's a way to get them to try, and enjoy, an old favorite.**

I pound lean ground beef or ground turkey
I egg
1/2 cup dry bread crumbs
1/2 cup chopped onion

1/2 cup spaghetti sauce
16 slices sandwich bread, 8 buns,
or 8 pita pockets

Preheat oven to 350°. Spray two mini loaf pans with cooking spray.
Combine all ingredients except bread in large bowl. Mix well. Form
meat mixture into loaf shapes and place in pans. Bake 30 minutes or
until done. Cool and refrigerate. Slice cold meat loaf and make sandwiches with your bread of choice.

Servings: 8
Calories: 326 • Protein: 19 grams • Carbohydrates: 36 grams • Fat: 11 grams
Exchanges: 2 1/2 bread, 2 meat, 1/2 fat

Tuna-Apple Sandwich

**A sandwich as easy and delicious as this one
can surely make your kids, and you, smile.**

6-ounce can tuna packed in water
I small apple, peeled and sliced in chunks

I tablespoon mayonnaise
6 slices sandwich bread

In small bowl, combine tuna, apple chunks, and mayonnaise. Mix
well. Spread mixture on bread.

Servings: 3
Calories: 276 • Protein: 19 grams • Carbohydrates: 35 grams • Fat: 6 grams
Exchanges: 2 bread, 1 meat, 1/2 fruit, 1/2 fat

Turkey Rolls

Let the kids fill and roll up these delightful sandwiches.
You'll be lucky to get them away from the kids and pack
them up for lunch.

2 flour tortillas
2 teaspoons mayonnaise
2 slices thinly sliced deli turkey

1/2 cup shredded lettuce
2 tablespoons shredded cheese,
  any type

Lay out tortillas. Spread with mayonnaise. Layer turkey slice, lettuce,
and cheese onto tortillas. Roll up and wrap.

Servings: 2
Calories: 218 • Protein: 14 grams • Carbohydrates: 20 grams • Fat: 9 grams
Exchanges: 1 bread, 1 meat, 1 fat

Garden Sandwich

This sandwich is so easy and so nutritious.
You can pack it into the entire family's lunch box.
If your kids don't like tomatoes, just leave them out.
You can also add lettuce and alfalfa sprouts if you like.

2 slices sandwich bread, any type
1 teaspoon margarine
4 slices cucumber, peeled

2 slices tomato
1 slice cheese, any type

Spread margarine on bread. Layer vegetables and cheese. Top with
remaining slice of bread.

Servings: 1
Calories: 265 • Protein: 9 grams • Carbohydrates: 32 grams • Fat: 11 grams
Exchanges: 2 bread, 1/2 meat, 1/2 vegetable, 1 1/2 fat

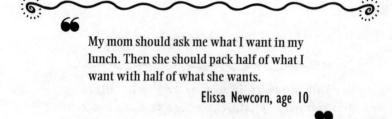

My mom should ask me what I want in my lunch. Then she should pack half of what I want with half of what she wants.

Elissa Newcorn, age 10

Non-Sandwich Favorites

Geez-O-Cheez Kabobs

Turkey on a Breadstick

Lunch on a Stick

Pasta with Artichokes and Cheese

Mini Drumsticks

Chicken Tabouleh Salad

Tortellini with Parmesan Cheese

I like it when my mom puts a lot of
different things in my lunch.

Melissa Gold, age 8

Geez-O-Cheez Kabobs

Your kids will have fun making and eating these mini-kabobs. Experiment with other versions of these, too.

20 1/2-inch cubes cheese (cheddar, brick, Muenster, Colby, Monterey Jack)
2 dill pickles, sliced into chunks

10 olives
1 stalk celery, sliced into chunks
10 toothpicks

Thread 2 cheese cubes and a pickle, olive, and piece of celery onto each toothpick. Continue until everything's used.

Servings: 10
Calories: 46 • Protein: 3 grams • Carbohydrates: 1 gram • Fat: 3 grams
Exchanges: 1/2 meat, 1/2 fat

Turkey on a Breadstick

Gobble this one up for lunch sometime.

2 slices deli-sliced turkey
2 teaspoons mustard, mayonnaise, or margarine

2 long hard breadsticks

Spread mustard, mayonnaise, or margarine on each slice of turkey. Roll turkey around top of breadstick, leaving a handle for grabbing. Dab a small amount of spread at seam of turkey to seal edge.

Servings: 2
Calories: 180 • Protein: 10 grams • Carbohydrates: 27 grams • Fat: 3 grams
Exchanges: 1 1/2 bread, 1/2 meat

Lunch on a Stick

Wouldn't your child love to find his lunch on a stick for a change? You can make it a surprise lunch treat or let him create his own.

4 cubes of cheese, any variety
4 chunks of fresh peppers, any variety
4 cherry tomatoes

4 melon balls, any variety
4 cubes cooked turkey, chicken, or ham
6 wooden toothpicks

Thread cheese, peppers, tomatoes, melon balls, and meats on toothpicks in whatever order you like.

Servings: 2
Calories: 105 • Protein: 9 grams • Carbohydrates: 5 grams • Fat: 6 grams
Exchanges: I meat, 1/2 vegetable, I fat

Pasta with Artichokes and Cheese

Pasta makes a great lunch; we just don't always think of it. Here's a recipe with room for lots of variations. Try adding tuna or chicken, too.

6-ounce jar marinated artichoke hearts
2 cups cooked pasta, any shape

1/4 cup shredded cheddar cheese
1/4 cup Italian salad dressing

Drain artichoke hearts. Combine drained artichoke hearts, pasta, and cheese in medium bowl. Toss well. Add dressing to pasta mixture. Toss gently.

If preparing the night before, separate servings into small airtight containers, and refrigerate.

Servings: 6
Calories: 158 • Protein: 4 grams • Carbohydrates: 16 grams • Fat: 9 grams
Exchanges: I bread, 1/2 vegetable, I 1/2 fat

Mini Drumsticks

Kids love drumsticks. These mini ones come from the upper part of the wing. They taste great cold and are easy to pack.

12 mini drumsticks (you can use regular drumsticks too, but fewer of them)
1/2 cup brown sugar

1/2 cup soy sauce
1/8 teaspoon ginger

Put drumsticks in large bowl or baking pan. Set aside. Combine remaining ingredients. Mix well. Pour marinade over chicken. Set in refrigerator. Marinate at least 30 minutes.

Preheat oven to 350°. Drain marinade from chicken, reserving marinade. Bake chicken for 20 to 30 minutes or until tender. Baste occasionally with marinade.

Servings: 6
Calories: 170 • Protein: 15 grams • Carbohydrates: 14 grams • Fat: 6 grams
Exchanges: 2 meat, 1 fruit

66 One day I took some leftover fried chicken to lunch. Everyone wanted my chicken. They would have traded cupcakes! One kid offered me a dollar.

Ross Whitehead, age 10 **99**

Chicken Tabouleh Salad

This Middle Eastern salad can be made in advance and refrigerated until you're ready to eat it. Actually, it tastes better after it is stored overnight because the bulgur soaks up the dressing.

1 cup cooked bulgur wheat
1 cup chopped cooked chicken
1 tomato, chopped
1/4 cup snipped parsley
1/4 cup chopped cucumber
2 tablespoons chopped green onion

1/4 cup oil
1/4 cup lemon juice
1 clove minced garlic
1/2 teaspoon salt
1/4 teaspoon pepper

Place cooked bulgur wheat in large bowl. Add chicken, tomato, parsley, cucumber, and onion.

In small container with lid or salad dressing jar, combine remaining ingredients. Shake dressing well. Pour dressing over bulgur mixture. Toss salad. Pack in airtight container and store in refrigerator until ready to use.

Servings: 6
Calories: 149 • Protein: 6 grams • Carbohydrates: 8 grams • Fat: 11 grams
Exchanges: 1/2 bread, 1/2 meat, 1/2 vegetable, 2 fat

Tortellini with Parmesan Cheese

Kids like eating tortellini with their fingers (a fork can be used too). They're as good cold as they are warm.

6 ounces frozen cheese tortellini
2 tablespoons margarine
2 tablespoons grated Parmesan cheese

Prepare tortellini according to package directions. Drain. Toss with margarine and Parmesan cheese. Refrigerate until ready to use.

Servings: 4
Calories: 146 • Protein: 6 grams • Carbohydrates: 8 grams • Fat: 10 grams
Exchanges: 1/2 bread, 1/2 meat, 1 1/2 fat

Sides to Go

Salad Mix-Ups

Fruit Salad Medley

Tropical Fruit Salad

Sweet Coleslaw

Italian Pasta Salad

Pickle Roll

Waldorf Salad

Carrot and Raisin Salad

Frosty Fruit Cocktail

Fresh Fruit on a Stick

Peanut Butter Dip

Dried Apples

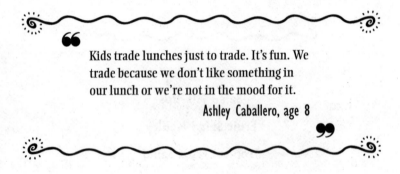

Kids trade lunches just to trade. It's fun. We trade because we don't like something in our lunch or we're not in the mood for it.

Ashley Caballero, age 8

Salad Mix-Ups

Try various options to make a salad of your choice. Your kids will have fun making up theirs, too. It's like making a brown-bag salad bar to go.

Start with lettuce, if you like, then add vegetables, extra protein, and toppings to go...

Choose Your Veggies	**Add Some Protein**	**Top It Off**
green pepper	turkey	alfalfa sprouts
yellow pepper	chicken	bean sprouts
red pepper	shredded cheese	croutons
cherry tomato	ham	sunflower seeds
carrot	tuna	raisins
celery	shrimp	chow mein noodles
radish	crabmeat	
zucchini	roast beef	
broccoli	boiled egg	
cauliflower	garbanzo beans	

Use individual-size packets of salad dressings to pack with your salad, too.

Fruit Salad Medley

This colorful salad pleases any appetite.
It's hard to believe how nutritious it really is.

11-ounce can mandarin oranges
2 cups sliced strawberries
1 cup sliced bananas

1/2 cup peeled and sliced apples
1 cup mini-marshmallows

Drain oranges, reserving liquid. In large bowl combine all ingredients, except marshmallows. Add liquid from oranges to mixture and toss. Cover and chill about an hour. Before serving, toss in marshmallows. (Keep marshmallows separate when packing for lunch and let your child mix them in.)

Servings: 6
Calories: 99 • Protein: 1 gram • Carbohydrates: 25 grams • Fat: 0
Exchanges: 1 1/2 fruit

Tropical Fruit Salad

When melons are in season this makes a great
take-along salad. It's fresh, sweet, and ever so tasty.

1/2 cup cantaloupe balls
1/2 cup watermelon balls
1/2 cup honeydew balls
1 kiwi, peeled and sliced
1/4 cup pineapple chunks

2 tablespoons shredded coconut
1/4 cup orange juice
1 tablespoon honey, optional
(use only if fruit isn't ripe
and sweet)

Combine fruit in large bowl. Pour orange juice (mixed with honey, if necessary) over top. Toss until well blended.

Servings: 4
Calories: 62 • Protein: 1 gram • Carbohydrates: 13 grams • Fat: 1 gram
Exchanges: 1 fruit

Sweet Coleslaw

**This easy slaw makes a big hit with the entire family.
Save some from dinner, and pack it up for tomorrow's lunch.**

1 1/2 cups shredded cabbage
1 cup shredded carrots
1/2 cup raisins
1/4 cup slivered almonds

1/2 cup vanilla yogurt
8-ounce can unsweetened pineapple
   tidbits, drained

In large bowl, combine all ingredients. Mix well.

Servings: 8
Calories: 89 • Protein: 2 grams • Carbohydrates: 16 grams • Fat: 2 grams
Exchanges: 1 fruit, 1/2 vegetable, 1/2 fat

Italian Pasta Salad

**This quick dish can be served as a side dish or main course.
You can even add some shredded cheese for extra zip.**

1 cup cooked pasta
1/2-pound bag frozen vegetables, cooked

1/4 cup Italian dressing

Combine cooked pasta and vegetables. Toss with Italian dressing.
Cover and chill until ready to use.

Servings: 4
Calories: 151 • Protein: 3 grams • Carbohydrates: 19 grams • Fat: 7 grams
Exchanges: 1/2 bread, 1 vegetable, 1 1/2 fat

Pickle Roll

Try this tasty, crunchy treat. You can prepare this ahead of time or pack the ingredients separately for the kids to wrap during lunch.

I slice American cheese   I dill pickle

Roll cheese around pickle.

> **Servings:** I
> **Calories:** 81 • **Protein:** 4 grams • **Carbohydrates:** 4 grams • **Fat:** 5 grams
> **Exchanges:** 1/2 meat, 1/2 vegetable, 1/2 fat

Waldorf Salad

This colorful, crunchy salad is a favorite of many kids. Let them help make it, too. They'll enjoy it even more.

2 red apples   1/2 cup chopped walnuts
2 tablespoons orange juice   1/2 cup raisins
2 stalks celery, chopped   1/4 cup mayonnaise

Core apples and chop into small pieces. Place in small bowl. Mix with orange juice to prevent them from turning brown. Combine remaining ingredients. Add apples. Mix well. Cool in refrigerator until ready to eat.

> **Servings:** 6
> **Calories:** 197 • **Protein:** 3 grams • **Carbohydrates:** 19 grams • **Fat:** 13 grams
> **Exchanges:** 1/2 meat, I fruit, 2 fat

Carrot and Raisin Salad

**This easy-to-prepare salad can be served with
dinner and then packed up for lunch the next day.
It's a tasty favorite for kids of all ages.**

2 carrots   2 tablespoons mayonnaise
1/2 cup raisins

Finely shred carrots. Combine carrots and raisins in medium bowl.
Add mayonnaise. Mix well. Refrigerate until ready to eat.

Servings: 4
Calories: 119 • Protein: 1 gram • Carbohydrates: 18 grams • Fat: 6 grams
Exchanges: 1 fruit, 1/2 vegetable, 1 fat

Frosty Fruit Cocktail

**This quick fruit treat is easy to put together.
Make several and keep them in the freezer until ready to use.
They can also serve as ice packs for your lunch.**

8-ounce can pineapple chunks,   1/4 teaspoon ground ginger
  packed in juice   3 cups sliced frozen or fresh
1/2 cup chopped walnuts   strawberries
2 tablespoons orange juice   1 cup frozen or fresh blueberries

In large bowl combine pineapple chunks (with juice), walnuts, orange
juice, and ginger. Toss to combine fruit and juices. Add berries. Toss
well. Divide fruit mixture into 4 equal servings and pack in airtight
plastic freezer containers. Freeze.

When packing for lunch, put freezer container in an insulated lunch
container. The fruit will partially thaw before lunchtime and remain
frosty and tasty.

Servings: 4
Calories: 181 • Protein: 5 grams • Carbohydrates: 23 grams • Fat: 9 grams
Exchanges: 1/2 meat, 1 1/2 fruit, 1 fat

Fresh Fruit on a Stick

For some reason, fruit tastes better on a stick than it does in a bowl. If you want your kids to enjoy their fruit, try this easy recipe. You can even have them prepare it themselves.

1/4 pound seedless grapes
1 cup pineapple chunks
3/4 cup strawberries

1/2 cup blueberries
1/2 cup raspberries
wooden skewers

Thread fruit on wooden skewers, alternating types of fruit.

Servings: 4
Calories: 79 • Protein: 1 gram • Carbohydrates: 20 grams • Fat: 0
Exchanges: 1 1/2 fruit

Peanut Butter Dip

Try this easy dip with raw vegetables or fresh fruit. It's easy to make and keeps well in a lunch box.

1/2 cup peanut butter   2 tablespoons honey

Combine ingredients. Mix well. Use for dipping fresh vegetable sticks and fresh fruit chunks.

Servings: 8
Calories: 110 • Protein: 4 grams • Carbohydrates: 8 grams • Fat: 8 grams
Exchanges: 1/2 meat, 1/2 fruit, 1 fat

Dried Apples

Dried apples can be bought at the store, but they are so much more fun to make. Share some time with your children and make some today. You may want to double or triple this recipe.

I 1/2 teaspoons lemon juice
I 1/2 tablespoons water

2 apples (Golden Delicious, McIntosh)

Combine lemon juice and water in a small bowl. Peel and core apples. Slice them into 1/8-inch rings. Drop apple rings into water mixture, then remove them. Pat dry with paper towels. Place apple rings on wire cooling racks.

To dry: Heat rings in 150° oven on wire cooling rack for about 4 hours. Be sure to turn once after 2 hours. Or string apples through their center with heavy string, and hang in a dry warm place (by the fireplace or a sunny window) for 1 to 2 weeks. Taste periodically to test for doneness.

When dry, store rings in an airtight container or plastic bag until ready to eat.

Servings: 2
Calories: 82 • Protein: 0 • Carbohydrates: 21 grams • Fat: 0
Exchanges: 1 1/2 fruit

66

I like it when my mom draws pictures on
my lunch bag.

Kyle Bernicky, age 9

99

I like it when my mom writes notes on my napkin.

Chloe Stein, age 7

Quick Breads and Starches

Peanut Butter
Chocolate Chip Muffins

Raisin Nut Bran Muffins

One Bowl Banana Bread

Very Berry Muffins

Fine French Toast

Alphabetter Muffins

Peanut Butter and Jam Muffins

Peanut Butter Banana Bread

Sweet Corn-Bread Muffins

Cranberry Bread

Raisin Bread

Zucchini Bread

Orange Oat Muffins

Peanut Butter Chocolate Chip Muffins

Make these in large or mini muffin tins, whatever you prefer. They make a treat your kids will enjoy over and over again.

1 1/2 cups flour
1/3 cup sugar
2 1/2 teaspoons baking powder
1/2 cup chunky peanut butter

2 tablespoons margarine
2 eggs, beaten
3/4 cup lowfat milk
1/2 cup semi-sweet chocolate chips

Preheat oven to 400°. Combine flour, sugar, and baking powder. Cut peanut butter and margarine into dry mixture until coarse crumbs appear. In small bowl combine eggs and milk. Add to flour mixture and stir until mixture is lumpy. Fold in chocolate chips. Set muffin papers in muffin tins, or spray tins with cooking spray. Drop batter into tins to 2/3 full. Bake 12 to 15 minutes until light brown. Cool.

Servings: 12 (1 dozen large muffins or 2 dozen mini-muffins)
Calories: 212 • Protein: 6 grams • Carbohydrates: 25 grams • Fat: 11 grams
Exchanges: 1 bread, 1/2 meat, 1/2 fruit, 1 1/2 fat

Raisin Nut Bran Muffins

A delicious way to get fiber into your child's diet.

2 cups raisin bran cereal
1 1/4 cups flour
1/2 cup sugar
1/2 cup chopped walnuts
1 teaspoon baking soda

1/2 teaspoon salt
1 egg
1 cup lowfat milk
1/4 cup oil

Preheat oven to 375°. In large bowl combine first 6 ingredients. Add remaining ingredients one at a time, stirring after each is added. Mix well, but do not overmix. Pour batter 2/3 full into muffin cups or into muffin tin sprayed with cooking spray. Bake 20 to 25 minutes.

Servings: 12
Calories: 197 • Protein: 4 grams • Carbohydrates: 27 grams • Fat: 9 grams
Exchanges: 1 bread, 1/2 fruit, 1 fat

One Bowl Banana Bread

This is one of Sandy's family's favorite recipes. Make use of your ripe bananas to try all the variations of this bread: try it plain, with nuts, or with chocolate chips. The bread freezes well, too.

3/4 cup sugar
1 1/2 cups mashed bananas
   (about 3 ripe bananas)
1/2 cup oil
2 eggs
2 cups flour
2 teaspoons vanilla

1 teaspoon baking soda
1/2 teaspoon baking powder
1/2 teaspoon salt
1/2 cup chopped nuts, optional
1/2 cup semi-sweet chocolate chips,
   if desired
Cooking spray

Preheat oven to 325°. Combine all ingredients in large bowl. Mix well. Spray 2 loaf pans with cooking spray. Pour batter into pans. Bake 50 to 60 minutes or until golden brown and top springs back when touched lightly with finger. Cool.

Servings: 24
Calories: 140 • Protein: 2 grams • Carbohydrates: 20 grams • Fat: 6 grams
Exchanges: 1/2 bread, 1/2 fruit, 1 fat

> I like breakfast for lunch. I bring cereal and buy milk at school.
>
> Cara Yaffe, age 6

Very Berry Muffins

These sweet blueberry muffins can be made
ahead of time, served for a breakfast on the run,
and packed for a healthy lunch, too.

2 cups flour
1 tablespoon baking powder
1/4 teaspoon salt
6 tablespoons margarine
3/4 cup sugar

2 eggs
1/2 cup lowfat milk
1 teaspoon vanilla
2 1/2 cups fresh blueberries

Preheat oven to 375°. In small bowl, combine flour, baking powder, and salt. Set aside.

In large bowl cream margarine and sugar. Add eggs, milk, and vanilla. Add dry mixture. Mix well. Fold blueberries into mixture. Spray muffin tins with cooking spray or line with paper liners. Pour batter 2/3 full into muffin cups. Bake 25 minutes or until light brown.

Servings: 12
Calories: 211 • Protein: 4 grams • Carbohydrates: 33 grams • Fat: 7 grams
Exchanges: 1 bread, 1 fruit, 1 fat

Fine French Toast

You might think French toast is just for breakfast,
but cold French toast makes a great lunch, too. You can
pack prepacked servings of syrup for dipping, too.

2 eggs
1/2 cup lowfat milk
1/2 teaspoon cinnamon
1/4 teaspoon vanilla

6 slices bread (white, whole wheat,
    French, sourdough, challah)
2 tablespoons margarine

In medium bowl, beat eggs. Add milk, cinnamon, and vanilla. Heat skillet over medium heat. Melt 1 tablespoon margarine in hot skillet. Dip bread into egg mixture to coat on both sides. Cook 3 slices of bread at a time, turning over after browned on bottom. Remove browned French toast after browned on both sides. Continue with remaining margarine and bread.

Servings: 6
Calories: 146 • Protein: 5 grams • Carbohydrates: 16 grams • Fat: 7 grams
Exchanges: 1 bread, 1/2 meat, 1 fat

Alphabetter Muffins

Start with A for apple, B for banana, and C for chocolate chips, and you have a delicious muffin treat.

1 3/4 cups flour
2 teaspoons baking powder
1/2 teaspoon baking soda
1 1/2 cups mashed bananas
(about 3 ripe bananas)

1/2 cup brown sugar
1/3 cup oil
1 egg
1 apple, peeled and chopped*
1/2 cup semi-sweet chocolate chips

Preheat oven to 350°. In large bowl, combine flour, baking powder, and baking soda. Add remaining ingredients. Mix well. Spray muffin tins with cooking spray or line with paper liners. Pour batter 2/3 full into muffin cups. Bake about 20 to 25 minutes until browned.

*if peeling ahead of time, mix apple chunks with 1 tablespoon lemon juice to keep from turning brown

Servings: 12
Calories: 214 • Protein: 3 grams • Carbohydrates: 32 grams • Fat: 9 grams
Exchanges: 1 bread, 1 fruit, 1 1/2 fat

66
My mom always keeps the crust on the bread of my sandwich even though I never eat it.

Emily Robin, age 9
99

Peanut Butter and Jam Muffins

We've hidden jam inside these muffins, but you can substitute blueberries or even a secret message instead if you like.

1 cup flour	1 egg
1/2 cup quick cooking oats	3/4 cup lowfat milk
1/4 cup sugar	1/2 cup peanut butter
2 teaspoons baking powder	3/4 cup jam or jelly, any flavor
1/2 teaspoon salt	

Preheat oven to 400°. In large bowl, combine flour, oats, sugar, baking powder, and salt. Add egg and milk. Stir just until mixed. Mixture will be lumpy. Spray muffin tins with cooking spray or line with paper liners. Pour batter 1/2 full into muffin cups. Drop about 1 teaspoon peanut butter and 1 tablespoon jam on batter in each cup. Cover filling until hidden with additional batter to fill cup about 2/3 full. Bake 20 to 25 minutes or until browned.

Servings: 12
Calories: 198 • Protein: 5 grams • Carbohydrates: 31 grams • Fat: 6 grams
Exchanges: 1/2 bread, 1/2 meat, 1/2 fruit, 1 fat

Peanut Butter Banana Bread

Delicious, nutritious, and full of protein, too.
The bananas add a flavorful touch, but you can also
make this bread without the bananas if you like.

1 1/2 cups flour	3/4 cup peanut butter
3/4 cup sugar	1 egg
2 teaspoons baking powder	1 cup mashed bananas (about
1/2 teaspoon baking soda	2 ripe bananas)
1/2 teaspoon salt	Cooking spray

Preheat oven to 350°. In small bowl, combine, flour, sugar, baking powder, soda, and salt.

In large bowl, combine remaining ingredients. Beat until smooth. Add dry mixture, and mix well. Spray loaf pan with cooking spray. Pour batter into loaf pan. Bake 55 to 60 minutes or until browned.

Servings: 12
Calories: 223 • Protein: 6 grams • Carbohydrates: 32 grams • Fat: 9 grams
Exchanges: I bread, 1/2 meat, I 1/2 fruit, I fat

Sweet Corn-Bread Muffins

A favorite with soup or chili, these muffins are also fun to make with your kids while sharing stories about Indians and early American pioneers.

1/2 cup flour
1/2 cup cornmeal
I teaspoon baking powder
1/2 teaspoon baking soda
3/4 cup brown sugar

1/4 cup lowfat milk
1/4 cup plain lowfat yogurt
I egg
2 tablespoons oil

Preheat oven to 400°. In large bowl, combine flour, cornmeal, baking powder, soda, and brown sugar. In small bowl, combine remaining ingredients. Add liquid mixture to dry mixture. Stir just until mixed. Spray muffin tins with cooking spray or line with paper liners. Pour batter 2/3 full into muffin tins. Bake 12 to 15 minutes or until browned.

Servings: 6
Calories: 207 • Protein: 4 grams • Carbohydrates: 35 grams • Fat: 6 grams
Exchanges: I bread, I fruit, I fat

Cranberry Bread

Not only is this easy-to-prepare bread great for lunch,
it also makes a great gift for teachers, counselors, and
bus drivers during the holiday season.

2 cups flour
1 cup sugar
1 1/2 teaspoons baking powder
1/2 teaspoon baking soda
1/2 teaspoon salt
1/4 cup margarine, softened

1 egg
1/2 cup orange juice
1/2 cup raisins
1 cup dried cranberries
Cooking spray

Preheat oven to 350°. In large bowl, combine flour, sugar, baking
powder, soda, and salt. Add margarine, egg, and orange juice. Mix
well. Fold in raisins and cranberries. Spray loaf pan with cooking
spray. Pour batter into pan. Bake 60 to 70 minutes or until browned.

Servings: 12
Calories: 238 • Protein: 3 grams • Carbohydrates: 47 grams • Fat: 4 grams
Exchanges: 1 bread, 2 fruit

Raisin Bread

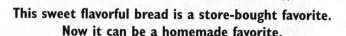

This sweet flavorful bread is a store-bought favorite.
Now it can be a homemade favorite.

2 cups flour
1/2 cup brown sugar
2 teaspoons baking powder
1 teaspoon salt
1 teaspoon cinnamon
1/4 teaspoon nutmeg

3/4 cup raisins
3/4 cup rolled oats
2 eggs, beaten
1 cup lowfat milk
Cooking spray

Preheat oven to 350°. Combine all ingredients in large bowl. Mix
well. Pour batter into loaf pan sprayed with cooking spray. Bake 1
hour or until browned.

Servings: 12
Calories: 168 • Protein: 5 grams • Carbohydrates: 33 grams • Fat: 2 grams
Exchanges: 1 bread, 1 fruit

Zucchini Bread

You can hide zucchini in this bread and your kids won't even know it. They'll ask for more, and you'll be delighted.

1 3/4 cups flour
3/4 cup sugar
2 eggs, beaten
1/2 cup oil
1 cup coarsely grated zucchini
1/4 cup chopped pecans or walnuts

1 teaspoon cinnamon
1/2 teaspoon vanilla
1/2 teaspoon baking soda
1/8 teaspoon baking powder
Cooking spray

Preheat oven to 350°. Combine all ingredients in large bowl. Mix well. Pour batter into loaf pan sprayed with cooking spray. Bake 1 hour or until browned.

Servings: 12
Calories: 227 • Protein: 3 grams • Carbohydrates: 27 grams • Fat: 12 grams
Exchanges: 1 bread, 1 fruit, 2 fat

Orange Oat Muffins

You'll enjoy this delicious twist to a plain oat muffin.
It goes great with lunch and makes a good snack, too.

1 cup flour
1 tablespoon baking powder
1/2 teaspoon salt
1/2 teaspoon baking soda
2 cups rolled oats

1 cup orange juice
1/3 cup honey
1 egg
3 tablespoons oil

Preheat oven to 425°. Combine flour, baking powder, salt, soda, and oats in large bowl. Combine orange juice, honey, egg, and oil in small bowl. Mix well. Add liquid mixture to dry mixture. Stir just until combined. Bake 15 minutes.

Servings: 12
Calories: 163 • Protein: 4 grams • Carbohydrates: 27 grams • Fat: 5 grams
Exchanges: 1 bread, 1/2 fruit, 1/2 fat

Snacks, Treats, and Finishing Touches

Chinese Crunch
Oriental Nut Mix
Homemade Potato Chips
Cinnamon-Raisin Bagel Chips
Soft Pretzels
Cheesy Pretzels
Peanut Butter Granola Mix
Cinnamon Chips
Beary Good Snack Mix
Peanut Buttered Popcorn
Parmesan Popcorn
My Own Trail Mix
Favorite Snack Mix
Shake and Take Snack Mix
Tortilla Chips
Applesauce Snack Cake

Chocolate Chip
Granola Cookies
No-Bake Granola
Coconut Nut Bars
Chocolate Chip
Zucchini Cookies
Gingerbread Squares
Vanishing Oatmeal Chipsters
Peanut Butter Cookies
Peanut-Butter
ChocolateChip Cookies
Oatmeal-Raisin Cookies
Zippy Lemon Squares
Peanut Butter Shake
Apple Fruit Leather
Applesauce Brownies

Chinese Crunch

Here's a crunchy treat you'll enjoy. Its Chinese touch
makes it a fun option for festive parties, too.

2 cups chow mein noodles
2 cups rice square cereal (like Rice Chex)
1/2 cup peanuts

1/4 cup oil
2 teaspoons soy sauce
1/8 teaspoon garlic powder

Preheat oven to 300°. Combine chow mein noodles, cereal, and
peanuts in 9"x13" baking pan. In small bowl, combine oil, soy sauce,
and garlic powder. Sprinkle over noodle mixture. Toss well to coat.
Bake 18 to 20 minutes, stirring every few minutes. Cool. Keep prepared mixture in airtight jar or container until ready to use.

Servings: 8
Calories: 198 • Protein: 4 grams • Carbohydrates: 14 grams • Fat: 15 grams
Exchanges: 1/2 bread, 1/2 meat, 2 1/2 fat

Oriental Nut Mix

Great for lunch or after-school snack, this treat
is one kids (and adults) will continue to request.

1 cup cashews
1/2 cup peanuts
1 cup sunflower seeds
1 tablespoon corn oil
2 teaspoons oriental sesame oil
   or peanut oil

2 teaspoons soy sauce
3/4 teaspoon sugar
1/4 teaspoon ginger
Cooking spray

Preheat oven to 300°. In large bowl combine all nuts and seeds. In
small bowl combine oils with remaining ingredients. Pour oil mixture over nut mixture. Stir to coat. Spray cookie sheet with cooking
spray. Spread nut mixture on cookie sheet. Bake 15 to 20 minutes,
stirring every few minutes, or until nuts are lightly toasted. Store in
airtight container.

Servings: 12
Calories: 184 • Protein: 6 grams • Carbohydrates: 7 grams • Fat: 16 grams
Exchanges: 1 meat, 1 1/2 fruit, 2 1/2 fat

Homemade Potato Chips

**Have you ever tried making your own chips?
They're as fun to make as they are to eat.**

3-4 potatoes, unpeeled
3 tablespoons oil
1/2 teaspoon salt

1/4 teaspoon garlic powder
1/4 teaspoon onion powder
1/4 teaspoon paprika

Preheat oven to 450°. Thinly slice potatoes. Combine remaining
ingredients in a large bowl. Add potatoes. Toss well. Spread potatoes
in single layer on one or two baking sheets. (If you need a second
cookie sheet, use it, as the potatoes will darken if left out in the air
too long.) Bake 10 to 12 minutes, until brown on one side. Turn potatoes over with tongs or spatula and cook another 10 minutes, until
brown on the other side.

> **Servings: 6**
> **Calories: 171 • Protein: 2 grams • Carbohydrates: 26 grams • Fat: 7 grams**
> **Exchanges: 1 1/2 bread, 1 1/2 fat**

Cinnamon-Raisin Bagel Chips

**Cinnamon bagels make great bagel chips, but other flavors
work well, too. Make a variety of chips for your pantry.**

1 cinnamon-raisin bagel, one or two days old

Preheat oven to 350°. Slice bagel in thin slices, about 1/4-inch thick.
Set slices on cookie sheet. Bake 10 to 12 minutes until crisp and
golden brown.

> **Servings: 1**
> **Calories: 155 • Protein: 6 grams • Carbohydrates: 31 grams • Fat: 1 gram**
> **Exchanges: 1 1/2 bread, 1/2 fruit**

Soft Pretzels

Soft pretzels make a great addition to any lunch. You can purchase frozen ones or make a batch of your own if you have a little extra time.

I package dry yeast	4 cups flour
I 1/2 cups warm water	Cooking spray
I teaspoon salt	I egg, beaten
I tablespoon sugar	Coarse or kosher salt

Preheat oven to 425°. In large metal bowl, dissolve yeast in warm water. Add salt and sugar. Add flour and knead until smooth. Break dough into small pieces. Roll into thin ropes. Twist into pretzel shapes or shapes of your own. Spray cookie sheet with cooking spray. Place pretzels onto cookie sheet. Brush with beaten egg and sprinkle generously with coarse or kosher salt. Bake 15 minutes.

Servings: 24
Calories: 82 • Protein: 3 grams • Carbohydrates: 17 grams • Fat: 0
Exchanges: 1 bread

Cheesy Pretzels

Add some cheese to soft pretzels and you have a fun, delicious treat. You can make an after-school project out of these.

I 1/2 cups flour	I teaspoon sugar
1/2 cup shredded cheddar cheese	1/2 teaspoon salt
2/3 cup lowfat milk	Cooking spray
2 tablespoons margarine	I egg, beaten
2 teaspoons baking powder	Coarse or kosher salt

Preheat oven to 400°. In large bowl, combine all ingredients except egg and coarse or kosher salt. Remove dough from bowl and knead for 1 to 2 minutes on lightly floured surface.

Break dough into pieces. Roll into thin ropes. Twist into pretzel shapes or other shapes. Spray cookie sheet with cooking spray. Place

pretzels onto cookie sheet. Brush dough with beaten egg. Sprinkle
with coarse salt. Bake 10 to 15 minutes or until browned.

Servings: 12 small or 6 large
Calories: 107 • Protein: 4 grams • Carbohydrates: 13 grams • Fat: 4 grams
Exchanges: 1 bread, 1/2 fat

Peanut Butter Granola Mix

**Try this nutritious homemade granola.
It will be a hit with everyone in your family.**

1/2 cup peanut butter
1 tablespoon honey
2 tablespoons oil
4 cups dry unsweetened cereal

1 cup shelled peanuts
1/4 cup sunflower seeds
1/4 cup raisins
1/4 cup chocolate chips

Preheat oven to 325°. Combine peanut butter, honey, and oil in
large saucepan over low heat. Heat and stir until blended. Add cereal,
peanuts and seeds. Mix well. Pour mixture into 9"x13" pan. Bake
5 minutes. Stir. Bake an additional 5 minutes. Cool. Stir in raisins
and chocolate chips. Store in airtight container.

Servings: 16
Calories: 174 • Protein: 6 grams • Carbohydrates: 12 grams • Fat: 12 grams
Exchanges: 1/2 bread, 1/2 meat, 1/2 fruit, 2 fat

My mom had special note pads made 'From
Mom' just to write lunchtime messages.

Lindsey Miller, age 6

Cinnamon Chips

**What a great way to make a delicious snack chip!
They're so easy and tasty, too.**

I prepared 9" pie crust, uncooked
Cooking spray
1/4 cup melted margarine

1/4 cup sugar
1/2 teaspoon cinnamon
1/4 teaspoon nutmeg

Preheat oven to 400°. Flatten out crust and cut into small pieces, any shape you desire. Place chips in single layer on cookie sheet sprayed with cooking spray. Brush pieces with melted margarine. Combine sugar, cinnamon, and nutmeg. Sprinkle over chips. Bake 10 minutes or until browned. Store in airtight container.

Servings: 12
Calories: 132 • Protein: 1 gram • Carbohydrates: 12 grams • Fat: 9 grams
Exchanges: 1/2 bread, 1 fat

Beary Good Snack Mix

**Take along this beary good snack wherever you go.
It's great for car rides, picnics, and of course, lunch.**

2 cups bear-shaped graham crackers
2 cups toasted oat cereal
1 cup honey roasted peanuts

1/2 cup raisins
1/2 cup chocolate chips

Combine all ingredients in large bowl or resealable bag. Mix well. Store in airtight container.

Servings: 12
Calories: 161 • Protein: 4 grams • Carbohydrates: 20 grams • Fat: 8 grams
Exchanges: 1/2 bread, 1/2 meat, 1 fruit, 1 1/2 fat

Peanut Buttered Popcorn

**Add a peanut butter touch to your popcorn.
It's great with a movie and great for a snack.**

2 quarts prepared popcorn   I tablespoon margarine
I tablespoon peanut butter

Pour prepared popcorn in large bowl. Melt peanut butter and margarine over low heat or in microwave. Pour over popcorn. Toss to coat. Store in an airtight container.

**Servings: 8
Calories: 55 • Protein: I gram • Carbohydrates: 7 grams • Fat: 3 grams
Exchanges: 1/2 bread**

Parmesan Popcorn

This popcorn makes a great afternoon snack, and if you are fortunate to have any left over, you can pack it for lunch tomorrow.

2 quarts prepared popcorn   2 tablespoons grated Parmesan cheese
2 tablespoons margarine, melted

Pour prepared popcorn in large bowl. Melt margarine over low heat or in microwave. Pour over popcorn. Add Parmesan cheese. Toss to coat. Store in an airtight container.

**Servings: 8
Calories: 63 • Protein: 2 grams • Carbohydrates: 6 grams • Fat: 4 grams
Exchanges: 1/2 bread**

My Own Trail Mix

This makes a great snack or treat to grab on the run
—in the car, off to soccer, or at the end of lunch.

1/4 cup raisins
1/4 cup peanuts
1/4 cup sunflower seeds, shelled

3 tablespoons coconut
1/4 cup chocolate chips

Combine all ingredients. Store in airtight container.

Servings: 4
Calories: 202 • Protein: 5 grams • Carbohydrates: 20 grams • Fat: 13 grams
Exchanges: 1/2 meat, 2 fruit, 2 fat

Favorite Snack Mix

Make a batch of this snack mix and keep it handy for snacks
as well as lunches. It's fun to make and more fun to eat.

2 1/2 cups toasted oat cereal
1 1/2 cups pretzel sticks
1 cup small fish or oyster crackers
1 cup peanuts

1 teaspoon soy sauce
2 teaspoons Worcestershire sauce
Cooking spray

Preheat oven to 275°. Combine all ingredients in large bowl. Mix
well. Pour mixture into 9"x13" pan sprayed with cooking spray. Bake
30 minutes, stirring occasionally. Cool. Store in airtight container.

Servings: 12
Calories: 130 • Protein: 5 grams • Carbohydrates: 13 grams • Fat: 7 grams
Exchanges: 1/2 bread, 1/2 meat, 1 fat

Shake and Take Snack Mix

**Your little ones will have a ball helping with this snack.
Just add all the ingredients to a bag or bowl, and shake.
There's no baking involved so it's ready in no time.**

1 1/2 cups small fish crackers, any flavor
1 1/2 cups round oyster crackers
1 cup pretzels, any shape

1/4 package dry buttermilk salad
dressing mix, do not prepare
1 tablespoon oil

Combine crackers and pretzels in large bowl or bag. Mix together salad dressing mix and oil. Pour dressing over dry ingredients. Toss or shake well. Store in airtight container.

Servings: 8
Calories: 145 • Protein: 3 grams • Carbohydrates: 20 grams • Fat: 6 grams
Exchanges: 1 bread, 1 fat

Tortilla Chips

**Homemade tortilla chips are easy to make
and taste great alone or with salsa.**

2 corn tortillas

1 1/2 teaspoons oil

Preheat oven to 400°. Cut tortillas into 8 wedges. Place on cookie sheet. Brush with oil. Bake 7 to 10 minutes or until crisp and browned.

Servings: 2
Calories: 97 • Protein: 2 grams • Carbohydrates: 14 grams • Fat: 4 grams
Exchanges: 1 bread, 1/2 fat

Applesauce Snack Cake

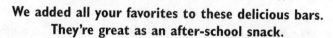

**Your kids can have their cake and eat it too.
They like the cake, you like the nutrition.**

1 1/4 cups flour
1/2 teaspoon baking soda
1/2 teaspoon cinnamon
1/4 cup margarine
1 egg, beaten

1/2 cup applesauce
1/3 cup light molasses
1/2 cup raisins
Cooking spray

Preheat oven to 350°. Combine flour, soda, and cinnamon in medium mixing bowl. Cut in margarine until mixture resembles coarse crumbs.

In small bowl, combine egg, applesauce, and molasses. Stir into flour mixture just until moistened. Add raisins. Spray an 8"x8" pan with cooking spray. Pour mixture into prepared pan. Bake for 25 to 30 minutes. Cool.

Servings: 16
Calories: 103 • Protein: 2 grams • Carbohydrates: 17 grams • Fat: 3 grams
Exchanges: 1/2 bread, 1/2 fruit

Chocolate Chip Granola Cookies

**We added all your favorites to these delicious bars.
They're great as an after-school snack.**

1 egg, beaten
3/4 cup oil
1/2 cup brown sugar
1/2 cup honey
1/4 cup water
1 teaspoon salt
1 teaspoon vanilla

3 cups quick-cooking rolled oats
1 cup whole wheat flour
3/4 cup wheat germ
1 cup chocolate chips
1/2 cup sunflower seeds
Cooking spray

Preheat oven to 350°. In small bowl combine egg, oil, brown sugar, honey, water, salt, and vanilla. In large bowl combine oats, flour, and wheat germ. Add liquid mixture to dry mixture and mix well. Stir in chocolate chips and sunflower seeds. Drop mixture by teaspoonfuls onto cookie sheet sprayed with cooking spray. Bake 15 to 20 minutes. Cool.

Servings: 24
Calories: 217 • Protein: 5 grams • Carbohydrates: 26 grams • Fat: 12 grams
Exchanges: 1 bread, 1 fruit, 2 fat

No-Bake Granola

**Here's a recipe you can turn over to the kids—
it's quick to make and there's no baking required.**

1 cup honey
1 cup peanut butter
2 1/2 cups rolled oats
1/2 cup chopped nuts

1/2 cup grated carrots
1/2 cup coconut
1/2 cup chocolate chips

Combine honey and peanut butter in large saucepan. Heat until melted. Remove from heat. Add oats, nuts, carrots, coconut, and chocolate chips. Mix well. Spread evenly in an ungreased 8"x8" square pan. Cool completely.

Servings: 16
Calories: 273 • Protein: 7 grams • Carbohydrates: 35 grams • Fat: 14 grams
Exchanges: 1/2 bread, 1/2 meat, 1 1/2 fruit, 2 fat

"

I like going shopping with my mom to pick
out what I want for lunch.

Jeff Pearl, age 9

"

Coconut Nut Bars

You may think you don't like coconut until you try these bars. They are chewy, flavorful, and delicious.

1 cup flour
1 teaspoon baking powder
1/4 cup margarine
1 cup brown sugar
1 egg

1/2 teaspoon vanilla
1/2 cup coconut
1/2 cup chopped nuts
Cooking spray

Preheat oven to 350°. Combine flour and baking powder in small bowl. Set aside. In medium saucepan, melt margarine. Remove from heat. Add brown sugar, egg, and vanilla. Mix well. Add flour mixture. Stir in coconut and nuts. Pour batter into an 8"x8" baking pan sprayed with cooking spray. Bake 20 to 25 minutes. Cool.

Servings: 25
Calories: 82 • Protein: 1 gram • Carbohydrates: 11 grams • Fat: 4 grams
Exchanges: 1/2 fruit, 1/2 fat

Chocolate Chip Zucchini Cookies

Here's a great way to hide the veggies. Keep it your little secret.

1/2 cup margarine, softened
1 cup sugar
1 egg
2 cups flour
1 teaspoon baking soda

1 teaspoon cinnamon
1/2 teaspoon salt
1 medium zucchini, grated (1 cup)
1 cup semi-sweet chocolate chips
Cooking spray

Preheat oven to 350°. In large bowl, cream margarine and sugar until light and fluffy. Add egg, flour, baking soda, cinnamon, and salt. Mix well. Add zucchini and chocolate chips. Spray cookie sheet with cooking spray. Drop cookie mixture by tablespoonfuls onto cookie sheets. Bake 15 to 20 minutes or until browned.

Servings: 4 dozen
Calories: 71 • Protein: 1 gram • Carbohydrates: 10 grams • Fat: 3 grams
Exchanges: 1/2 bread, 1/2 fruit

Gingerbread Squares

The entire family will enjoy this old American favorite.

1/2 cup sugar
1 teaspoon cinnamon
1/2 teaspoon nutmeg
1/4 teaspoon cloves
1 egg
1/4 cup oil

1 cup honey
1 cup lowfat yogurt
2 cups flour
2 teaspoons baking soda
Cooking spray

Preheat oven to 325°. Combine sugar, cinnamon, nutmeg, and cloves. Beat in egg and oil. Add honey and yogurt. Mix well. Combine flour and soda. Add to batter. Mix well. Pour batter into an 8"x8" pan sprayed with cooking spray. Bake 45 to 50 minutes or until top springs back when touched lightly with finger.

Servings: 25
Calories: 122 • Protein: 2 grams • Carbohydrates: 24 grams • Fat: 3 grams
Exchanges: 1/2 bread, 1 fruit, 1/2 fat

Vanishing Oatmeal Chipsters

Make these in the morning. Watch them vanish throughout the day.

1 cup margarine or butter
1 cup sugar
1/2 cup brown sugar
2 eggs
2 teaspoons vanilla

1 1/3 cups flour
1 teaspoon salt
2 cups rolled oats
1 teaspoon baking soda
1 cup chocolate chips

Preheat oven to 350°. Combine margarine, sugars, eggs, and vanilla. Gradually add dry ingredients and chocolate chips. Drop by spoonfuls onto ungreased cookie sheet, and bake 8 to 10 minutes.

Servings: 4 dozen
Calories: 102 • Protein: 1 gram • Carbohydrates: 13 grams • Fat: 5 grams
Exchanges: 1/2 bread, 1/2 fruit, 1 fat

Peanut Butter Cookies

There are so many ways to bring peanut butter into a lunch. If you're not too tired of it yet, try these yummy, nutritious cookies.

1 cup flour
1 teaspoon baking powder
1/2 teaspoon baking soda
1/4 teaspoon salt
1/2 cup peanut butter
1/4 cup margarine, softened

1/2 cup sugar
1/2 cup brown sugar
1 egg
1 teaspoon lowfat milk
2 teaspoons vanilla

Preheat oven to 350°. In small bowl, combine flour, baking powder, soda, and salt. In large bowl, combine remaining ingredients. Mix until smooth. Combine dry mixture with peanut butter mixture. Mix well. Drop batter by tablespoonfuls onto ungreased cookie sheets. Bake 12 to 15 minutes or until browned.

Servings: 3 dozen
Calories: 66 • Protein: 1 gram • Carbohydrates: 8 grams • Fat: 3 grams
Exchanges: 1/2 fruit, 1/2 fat

"I don't like fruit surprises in my lunch. I also don't like the same thing two days in a row.

Stephanie Brontman, age 9"

Peanut Butter
Chocolate Chip Cookies

**Peanut butter finds its way into these yummy cookies
and helps make them more nutritious.**

1/2 cup peanut butter	1 teaspoon vanilla
1/2 cup margarine	1 cup flour
1/2 cup sugar	1 teaspoon baking soda
2/3 cup brown sugar	1/2 teaspoon cinnamon
1 egg	1/2 cup chocolate chips

Preheat oven to 350°. Cream peanut butter, margarine, and sugars
together. Add remaining ingredients. Mix well. Drop by tablespoonfuls
onto ungreased cookie sheet. Bake 8 to 10 minutes until browned.

Servings: 2 1/2 dozen
Calories: 109 • Protein: 2 grams • Carbohydrates: 12 grams • Fat: 6 grams
Exchanges: 1/2 fruit, 1/2 fat

Oatmeal-Raisin Cookies

**This old standby recipe is a wholesome cookie
that kids will gobble up.**

1 cup flour	2/3 cup sugar
1/2 teaspoon salt	1 egg
1 teaspoon baking soda	2 tablespoons lowfat milk
1/2 teaspoon cinnamon	1 cup raisins
1/2 cup margarine	2 cups rolled oats
1/2 cup brown sugar	

Preheat oven to 375°. Combine flour, salt, soda, and cinnamon in
large bowl. Add remaining ingredients, mixing well. Drop by tablespoonfuls onto ungreased cookie sheet. Bake 10 to 12 minutes or
until browned.

Servings: 4 dozen
Calories: 67 • Protein: 1 gram • Carbohydrates: 11 grams • Fat: 2 grams
Exchanges: 1/2 bread, 1/2 fruit

Zippy Lemon Squares

**Zip up your lunch with this delightful treat.
It will hit the spot any day.**

1 cup flour
1/2 cup oil
1/4 cup powdered sugar
3/4 cup sugar
2 teaspoons grated lemon peel

2 tablespoons lemon juice
1/2 teaspoon baking powder
1/4 teaspoon salt
2 eggs

Preheat oven to 350°. Combine flour, oil, and powdered sugar in small bowl. Mix well. Press dough evenly with hands into the bottom of an ungreased 8"x8" pan. Dough should come up the sides about 1/2 inch. Bake 20 minutes.

Beat remaining ingredients together in small bowl until light and fluffy. Pour over hot crust. Bake just until there is no indentation in the center when touched lightly (about 20 minutes). Let stand and cool, then cut into squares.

Servings: 25
Calories: 90 • Protein: 1 gram • Carbohydrates: 11 grams • Fat: 5 grams
Exchanges: 1/2 fruit, 1 fat

Peanut Butter Shake

Sometimes your child may be in the mood for something different. Make this shake, store it in a thermos, and carry it off to school. It's fun to sip and healthy, too.

3 cups lowfat milk
1/4 cup peanut butter

3 tablespoons honey
1/2 teaspoon vanilla

Blend all ingredients together. Refrigerate or keep cool until ready to drink.

Servings: 4
Calories: 235 • Protein: 10 grams • Carbohydrates: 25 grams • Fat: 11 grams
Exchanges: 1/2 meat, 1 fruit, 1 milk, 2 fat

Apple Fruit Leather

We are always buying fruit leather because the kids like it so much. Did you ever consider trying to make your own? It's much more nutritious than store-bought leather.

1 1/2 cups applesauce (Other fruits like cherries, peaches, pears, pineapple, plums, and strawberries can be used too. Place fruit in a blender to create puree.)

Preheat oven to 400°. Spray cookie sheet with cooking spray. Spread applesauce evenly over cookie sheet. Place in oven. Reduce oven temperature to 200°. Bake about 3 hours or until applesauce isn't sticky and can be peeled off the cookie sheet. Remove from oven. Cut into 4"x4" squares with scissors. Store in airtight container.

Servings: 4
Calories: 39 • Protein: 0 • Carbohydrates: 10 grams • Fat: 0
Exchanges: 1 fruit

Applesauce Brownies

No one will ever know you added applesauce to these delicious brownies. It will make you enjoy serving them even more.

4 ounces unsweetened baking chocolate
1/2 cup applesauce
2 eggs
2 cups sugar
1/3 cup oil
1 teaspoon vanilla
1 cup flour
Cooking spray

In small saucepan, melt chocolate over low heat. Let cool about 20 minutes. Preheat oven to 350°. In large bowl, combine melted chocolate, applesauce, eggs, sugar, oil, and vanilla. Mix well. Gently mix flour into chocolate mixture until well blended. Spray a 9"x13" pan with cooking spray. Pour batter into prepared pan. Bake 25 minutes or until top springs back when touched lightly with finger.

Servings: 24
Calories: 144 • Protein: 2 grams • Carbohydrates: 23 grams • Fat: 6 grams
Exchanges: 1 fruit, 1 fat

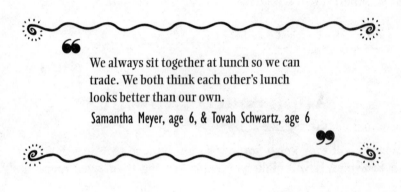

We always sit together at lunch so we can trade. We both think each other's lunch looks better than our own.

Samantha Meyer, age 6, & Tovah Schwartz, age 6

Index

Sweet Corn-Bread Muffins, 71

Also from
C H R O N I M E D   P U B L I S H I N G

Quick Meals for Healthy Kids and Busy Parents
Wholesome Family Recipes in 30 Minutes or Less
Sandra K. Nissenberg, M.S., R.D., Margaret L. Bogle, Ph.D., R.D.,
and Audrey C. Wright, M.S., R.D.

From three leading dietitians, who are also busy working mothers (Audrey Wright is president of The American Dietetic Association Foundation), here's the cookbook for parents who don't have much time to cook. This easy-to-use cookbook provides expert advice and a collection of healthy recipes for dishes that kids will want again and again. Most recipes take less than 30 minutes to prepare and include complete nutrition information.

Paper, 252 pages, 1-56561-064-4, $12.95

How Should I Feed My Child?
From Pregnancy to Preschool
Sandra K. Nissenberg, M.S., R.D., Margaret L. Bogle, Ph.D., R.D.,
Edna P. Langholz, M.S., R.D., and Audrey C. Wright, M.S., R.D.

Addressing real issues and parents' most common concerns, this guide tells how to start your child off to a lifetime of good eating habits. Includes over 50 recipes for healthy and delicious kids' favorites. "From four nutrition experts with impressive credentials, the book offers easy-to-read, practical advice."—*USA Today*

Paper, 192 pages, 1-56561-035-0, $12.95

The Quality Time Family Cookbook
Over 200 Delicious, Healthy, and Fast Family Favorites
for Making Mealtime Creative and Fun
Julie Metcalf Cull, R.D.

A recent *Reader's Digest* poll revealed that children who eat four or more meals each week with their families score 18% higher in academic tests compared with those who dine with their families less often. But it's not enough simply to eat together; mealtime can be so much more. This revolutionary cookbook looks at improving the quality of family meals through creative but simple planning—while increasing nutrition value and decreasing the cost.

Paper, 320 pages, 1-56561-066-0, $12.95

200 Kid-Tested Ways to Lower the Fat in Your Child's Favorite Foods
How to Make the Brand-Name and Homemade Foods Your Kids Love More Healthful—and Delicious
Elaine Moquette-Magee, M.P.H., R.D.

Many of the foods available to kids, from breakfast cereals to school lunches, are loaded with fat. Now, here's a collection of useful advice and tips on reducing the fat and cholesterol in these foods—without your kids even noticing.

Paper, 336 pages, 1-56561-034-2, $12.95

The Healthy Start Kids Cookbook
Edited by Sandra K. Nissenberg, M.S., R.D.

This illustrated cookbook shows 6 to 10 year olds that making the food they love can be as fun as eating it. With a little help from an adult, children can create more than 70 delicious, easy, and imaginative concoctions that are surprisingly good for them. "Lively and kid-friendly, (this book) incorporates all the elements of healthful eating into a simple guide for kids."—Mindy Hermann, R.D., Consulting Nutrition Editor, *Child Magazine*

Paper, 192 pages, 1-56561-054-7, $9.95

To Order

Mark the book(s) you would like sent to you. Send a check or money order—no cash or CODs. (Please add $3.00 to the total price to cover postage and handling. Minnesota residents, add 6.5% sales tax. Prices are subject to change without notice.) Allow four to six weeks for delivery. Quantity discounts available upon request. Enclosed is _____.

Send your order to
Chronimed Publishing
PO Box 59032, Minneapolis, MN 55459-0032

Name _____

Address _____

City _____ State ____ ZIP _____

Phone _____

Or order by phone: **1-800/848-2793** (513-6475 in the Minneapolis/St Paul area). Please have your credit card number ready.